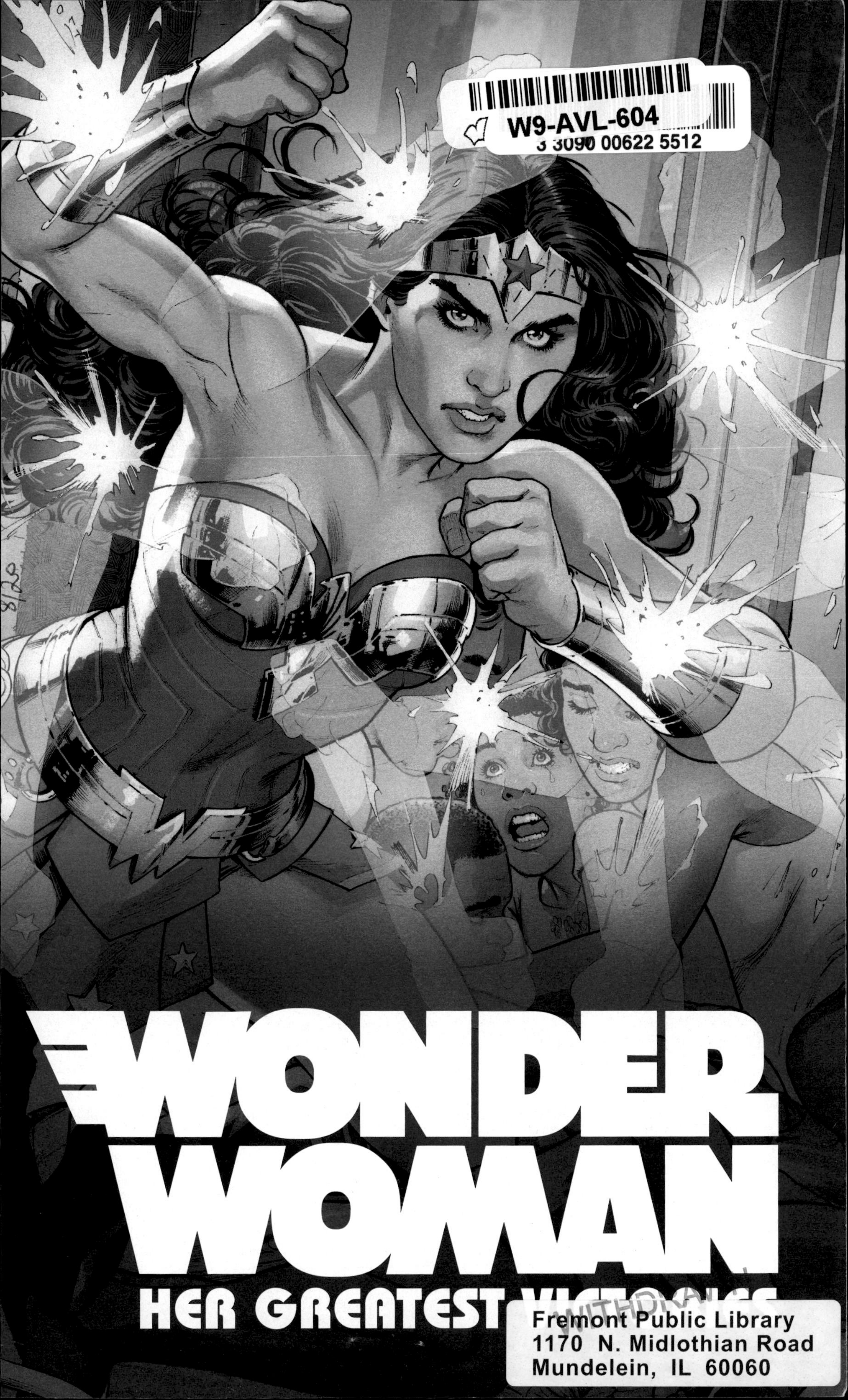
WONDER
WOMAN
HER GREATEST

WONDER WOMAN: HER GREATEST VICTORIES



DC Comics, 2900 West Alameda Ave., Burbank, CA 91505
Printed by LSC Communications, Kendallville, IN, USA. 3/20/20. First Printing.
ISBN: 978-1-4012-9434-2 | Walmart Edition ISBN: 978-1-77950-611-5

Library of Congress Cataloging-in-Publication Data is available.

# WONDER WOMAN

## HER GREATEST VICTORIES

WONDER WOMAN created by WILLIAM MOULTON MARSTON

SUPERMAN created by JERRY SIEGEL and JOE SHUSTER
By special arrangement with the Jerry Siegel family

# TABLE OF CONTENTS

WONDER WOMAN #49 variant cover by JENNY FRISON

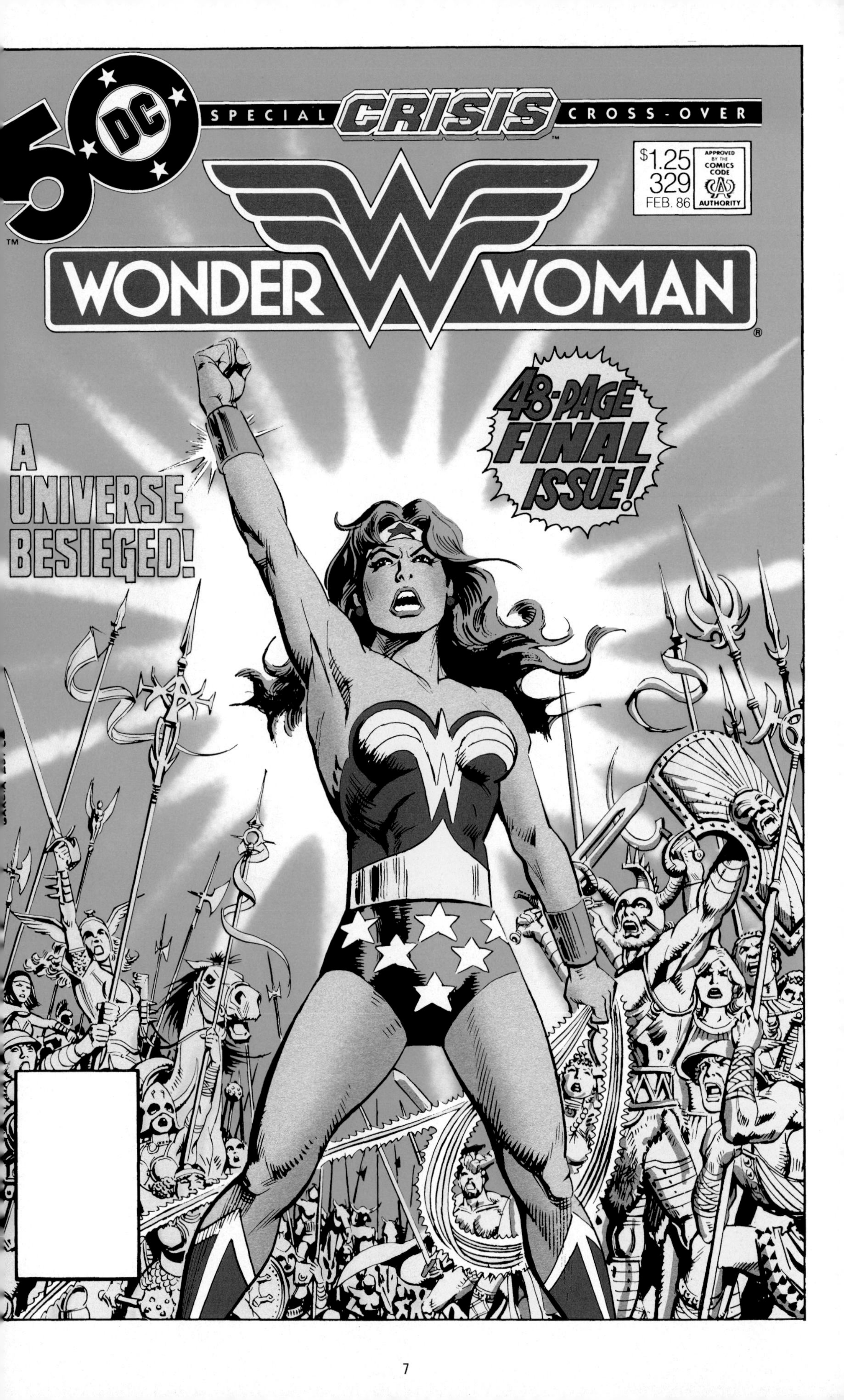
SPECIAL CRISIS CROSS-OVER
$1.25
329
FEB. 86
APPROVED BY THE COMICS CODE AUTHORITY
WONDER WOMAN
48-PAGE FINAL ISSUE!
A UNIVERSE BESIEGED!

PROLOGUE:
A PLACE THAT IS NOT A PLACE.
THEN WE ARE AGREED, LORD OF SHADES?
AGREED! I WILL PROVIDE YOU WITH THE WARRIORS YOU WANT...
...AND YOU WILL REPAY ME WITH HALF YOUR NEW-WON KINGDOM!
AN HONEST BARGAIN FOR US BOTH, O PRINCE OF MOLES!
YOU TREAD HEAVILY UPON MY GOOD WILL, ARES! NEVER MOCK ME!
WE ARE ALLIES, YOU AND I... BUT I AM NOT YOUR FRIEND.
TILL TONIGHT, HADES!
AYE, TILL TONIGHT.
A SWAGGERING FOOL--BUT HE'S USEFUL TO ME YET!
SOON, WITH PLEASURE, I WILL WATCH YOU DESTROY HIM!
G-2035
END OF PROLOGUE...
1

PARADISE ISLAND.
THE FIRES ARE BURNING OUT, BUT THE SCENT OF SMOKE REMAINS... A GRIM REMINDER OF BATTLE, IN A WAR THAT MIGHT NOT BE WON...
MOTHER, YOU MUST GO ON. WE CAN'T STOP FIGHTING NOW.
NOT JUST PARADISE ISLAND... NOT JUST OUR WORLD... THE ENTIRE UNIVERSE IS AT STAKE!
THEN WHAT MUST BE, MUST BE.
ALL MY LIFE I HAVE STRUGGLED WITH DESTINY, DIANA.
OF GODS AND MEN
2

BUT THOSE WHO DEFY DESTINY ARE DESTROYED.
LOOK ABOUT YOU, DAUGHTER. ADMIT THE TRUTH OF WHAT YOUR EYES TELL YOU. THE AMAZON ADVENTURE IS FINISHED.
THE DREAM IS DEAD.
A FINAL ADVENTURE OF
WONDER WOMAN
GERRY CONWAY WRITER
DON HECK ARTIST
HELEN VESIK LETTERER
NANSI HOOLAHAN COLORIST
ALAN GOLD EDITOR
3

NO. I WON'T ACCEPT IT.
YOU TAUGHT ME TO CHALLENGE DESTINY. MY WHOLE LIFE IS A DEFIANCE OF FATE! HOW CAN YOU TURN YOUR BACK ON THOSE LESSONS NOW?
I KNOW WHAT I KNOW.
WASN'T IT I WHO STOLE YOUR MEMORIES OF THE FIRST STEVE TREVOR... AN ACT THAT DEFIED FATE?
I THOUGHT I SPARED YOU NEEDLESS PAIN.
INSTEAD, I DROVE A WEDGE BETWEEN US THAT YET KEEPS US APART.
AND THIS... THE DESTRUCTION WE HAVE SUFFERED AT THE HANDS OF THOSE SHADOW CREATURES...*
...THIS IS MY FINAL PUNISHMENT.
I HAVE BROUGHT RUIN UPON MY SISTERS, I HAVE LOST THE CHILD OF MY HEART. I... CANNOT GO ON.
DEATH WILL BE A BLESSED RELEASE.
*WW #328--ALAN.
4

YOU WOULD NOT SAY SO, IF YOU KNEW THE SORROW OF HADES' KINGDOM.
I KNOW... I WHO SPENT HALF OF EVERY YEAR IN HIS COLD EMBRACE, RETURNING TO THE WORLD OF LIGHT ONLY AT WINTER'S END!
DEATH IS NO "RELEASE," HIPPOLYTA, QUEEN OF THE AMAZONS.
IT IS A WAITING WITHOUT END.
OR SO IT WAS, TILL THE UNDERWORLD FELL TO THE ANTI-MONITOR'S DARK LEGION. NOW THE DAMNED ARE TWICE DAMNED. AND HADES, MY HUSBAND, IS IN THRALL TO A SHADOW GREATER THAN HIS OWN.
YOU'LL FIND NO SUCCOR, THERE, HIPPOLYTA.
YOU'VE HEARD KORE, MOTHER. YOU KNOW SHE'S RIGHT. WHATEVER HAPPENED BETWEEN US, WHATEVER FEELINGS WE HAVE... WE MUST DEAL WITH IT HERE, IN THIS LIFE.
YOU SAY YOU'VE LOST MY LOVE, BUT THAT ISN'T TRUE.
I LOVE YOU, MOTHER... MORE THAN EVER NOW, WHEN WE FACE OUR GREATEST CHALLENGE. AND IF YOU TRULY LOVE ME...
5

...YOU'LL RALLY THE AMAZONS AS ONLY YOU CAN... AND LEAD US ALL INTO BATTLE!
HOW DID YOU BECOME SO STRONG? WHERE IS THE CHILD I HELD UPON MY KNEE?
I GREW UP, MOTHER. I'M THE WOMAN YOU MADE ME. BUT I'M ALSO THE CHILD WHO WILL ALWAYS NEED YOUR LOVE.
HELP ME.
MY QUEEN...
...OUR MASTER REQUIRES YOUR DEATH...
6

SWWAKK
SWWIIKK
7

DAUGHTER! ALL AROUND YOU--
ENOUGH!
WARRIORS OF THE UNDERWORLD, HEAR THE VOICE OF YOUR MISTRESS!
"I TELL YOU... CEASE THIS ATTACK...
"...RETURN TO YOUR PLACE OF MEMORIES AND YEARNING...
"YOUR TIME IN THE WORLD OF POSSIBILITIES IS OVER!
"LEAVE THE DARKNESS NEVERMORE."
9

LIKE PUPPETS SUDDENLY UNSTRUNG, THE AMAZON DEAD DROP TO THE RUBBLED EARTH, AS THEIR LIVING SISTERS LOOK ON--NOT WITHOUT A COLLECTIVE SHUDDER OF HORROR...
KORE, WHAT EVIL WAS THIS? WHOSE HAND STIRRED OUR FALLEN SISTERS AGAINST US?
ONLY ONE BEING CAN RELEASE THE INMATES OF ETERNITY: MY ERSTWHILE HUSBAND, THE LORD OF THE UNDERWORLD... HADES.
BUT YOU SAID THE UNDERWORLD HAD FALLEN TO THE ANTI-MONITOR.
EXACTLY. MY HUSBAND HAS TAKEN AN ALLY EVEN MORE HOSTILE THAN HE TO THE WORLD OF THE LIVING.
HADES IN LEAGUE WITH THE ANTI-MONITOR?
WHAT WILL THEY DO?
IF I KNOW MY HUSBAND... AND AFTER A NEAR ETERNITY, I THINK I DO... ATTACK ON PARADISE ISLAND WAS NOTHING MORE THAN AN AFTERTHOUGHT.
HIS TRUE TARGET REMAINS WHAT IT HAS ALWAYS BEEN, SINCE HE AND HIS BROTHERS OVERTHREW THE ANCIENT TITANS AND DIVIDED UP THE KINGDOMS OF THE UNIVERSE...
...MOUNT OLYMPUS, HOME OF THE GODS!

WASHINGTON, D.C.
NOT EVEN THE CAPITAL OF THE WORLD'S MOST POWERFUL NATION IS SAFE FROM THE RAVAGES OF A WORLD GOING MAD...
...FOR WHAT ARE NATIONS AND WORLDS, WHEN ENTIRE UNIVERSES MAY BE SWALLOWED BY DESTRUCTION?
YET HUMANKIND IS NOTHING IF IT IS NOT DEFIANT IN THE FACE OF DESTINY!
DON'T LET GO!
FOR GOD'S SAKE, LIEUTENANT-- YOU'VE GOT TO HANG ON!
COLONEL TREVOR I--I CAN'T!
OH, GOD--MY FINGERS ARE SO BLOODY--THEY'RE SLIPPING ON THE ROPE--
11

--I CAN'T HOLD ON--!
EEEEEEEEEEEEEEEEE
LAUREN!
THOOOOOM
12

COLONEL TREVOR!
I HEARD HIS VOICE, ETTA-- EVEN OVER THE NOISE OF THE STORM!
HE'S HERE SOMEWHERE! WE HAVE TO KEEP LOOKING EVEN IF--
THERE HE IS! COLONEL! COLONEL TREVOR!
BOY, ARE WE GLAD TO FIND YOU. EVERYTHING'S GOING CRAZY!
HAVE YOU SEEN LIEUTENANT HALEY? SHE RAN THIS WAY WHEN THE STORM BROKE, AND WE THOUGHT...
LAUREN HALEY IS DEAD. SHE STUMBLED... FELL INTO THAT CREVICE...
I COULDN'T SAVE HER. I HARDLY EVEN KNEW THE WOMAN... AND SHE'S DEAD.
UH... COLONEL...
...SHE ISN'T THE ONLY ONE. EVER SINCE WONDER WOMAN--UH, I MEAN, MAJOR PRINCE--TOOK OFF AFTER THOSE WEAPONERS, THINGS HAVE GOTTEN WEIRD-- AND DEADLY. *
THAT STORM STARTED FIRST, THEN THE EARTHQUAKES... AND THINGS STARTED EXPLODING. PEOPLE ARE DYING ALL OVER THE PENTAGON.
*AS TOLD LAST ISSUE--ALAN.
HE KNOWS THAT... HE'S BEEN TRYING TO HELP. HE'S BEEN EVERYWHERE, ALL OVER THE COMPOUND... TRYING TO SAVE PEOPLE...
BUT IT'S NO GOOD, COLONEL! WE'VE HEARD THROUGH THE DEFENSE NETWORK, IT ISN'T JUST WASHINGTON! THE WORLD IS COMING APART...!
13

WE THOUGHT, IF YOU COULD REACH DIANA PRINCE-- WONDER WOMAN--
SHE COULD DO SOMETHING.
I WISH I KNEW WHERE SHE WAS, ETTA.
SHE HASN'T ONCE LEFT MY THOUGHTS SINCE THIS MADNESS BEGAN...
NOR HAVE YOU LEFT MINE, STEVE TREVOR.
ANGEL.
14

YOU ARE AN ANGEL.
STEVE... WE'VE BEEN FOOLS FOR TOO LONG.
PLAYING AT LOVE LIKE CHILDREN... WHEN LIFE IS SO SHORT.
15

IF WE EVER HAVE THE CHANCE AGAIN... I WANT US TO SEAL OUR LOVE, AS MAN AND WOMAN.
WHAT DO YOU MEAN "IF WE EVER HAVE THE CHANCE AGAIN..."?
THE GODS ARE AT WAR, MY DARLING... THE GODS, AND THOSE WHO MAY BE GREATER THAN THE GODS. LOOK AROUND YOU.
THIS IS JUST A SHADOW OF WHAT THE GODS FACE ABOVE...
"WHAT IF EARTH BE BUT THE SHADOW OF HEAVEN, AND THINGS THEREIN...
"EACH TO OTHER LIKE, MORE THAN ON EARTH IS THOUGHT?"
MILTON. "PARADISE LOST."
16

HEY, I WASN'T BORN A SENATOR'S AIDE. BACK IN COLLEGE I ALMOST MAJORED IN THE CLASSICS.
CALL ME A ROMANTIC, BUT IN MY HEART I ALWAYS HAD A SOFT SPOT FOR LUCIFER...
YOU KNOW... "BETTER TO REIGN IN HELL THAN SERVE IN HEAV'N"?
HADES WOULD HAVE APPROVED OF LUCIFER, HOWARD. BUT NOW HE PLANS TO DO THE FALLEN ANGEL ONE BETTER.
HE'LL RULE IN HELL AND HEAVEN BOTH--
--UNLESS THE AMAZONS FIND THE STRENGTH TO STOP HIM!
GREAT WHEN DO WE LEAVE?
WHAT--?
YOU DIDN'T REALLY THINK I'D LET YOU OUT OF MY SIGHT, ESPECIALLY AFTER THAT SPEECH ABOUT LOVE--
--NOW DID YOU?
NOT REALLY. BUT I WOULDN'T ASK. IT HAD TO BE YOUR CHOICE.
WHAT CHOICE? YOU'RE THE WOMAN I LOVE. NOW LET'S GET THE HELL OUT OF HERE. NO PUN INTENDED.
17

HOWARD, DO YOU BELIEVE IN PREMONITIONS?
SURE. I KNEW WE WERE GOING TO FALL IN LOVE THE FIRST TIME I LAID EYES ON YOU. THAT'S A PREMONITION, AND IT CAME TRUE.
I HAVE A FEELING WE'LL NEVER SEE THEM AGAIN.
BUT I'M NOT SAD...
"...BECAUSE SOMEHOW, NO MATTER WHAT HAPPENS, I THINK THEY HAVE A CHANCE TO BE HAPPY TOGETHER AT LAST..."
18

HAT'S THE
LAN OF
TTACK,
IANA?
MOTHER AND THE AMAZONS AWAIT MY SIGNAL--WHICH I'LL GIVE ONCE I'VE SCOUTED OUT OLYMPUS. IN THE MEAN-TIME, THE GODDESS KORE WILL TRY TO ENLIST ATALANTA AND HER MORTAL AMAZONS FROM SOUTH AMERICA IN OUR CAUSE.
IF HADES IS INDEED RAISING THE DEAD TO WAR AGAINST THE GODS, WE WILL NEED EVERY FIGHTER WE CAN FIND.
DIANA--WHAT OES ON HERE? IS THIS OLYMPUS?
WHERE IS EVERYBODY?
I DON'T KNOW. I THOUGHT THE WAR MIGHT HAVE BEGUN BY NOW...
THE WAR HAS BEGUN, DAUGHTER OF HIPPOLYTA!
THE WAR HAS BEEN FOUGHT-- AND WON!
KKRUNNCH
19

ARES, GOD OF WAR, IS MASTER IN OLYMPUS NOW!
STEVE! MY HAND--
--GRAB MY HAND!
OKAY, ANGEL, I'VE GOT YOU, AND YOU'VE GOT ME--
--NOW WHAT DO WE DO?
THE CHOICE IS SIMPLE, MORTAL MAN!
SWEAR ALLEGIANCE TO ARES-- OR DIE!
IF YOU DON'T MIND, I CHOSE A THIRD PATH...
...DEFIANCE!
20

HOW DID YOU DO THAT?
YEARS OF PRACTICE.
OF COURSE, IT HELPS IF YOU'RE BORN AN AMAZON!
NO!
NOOOOOO
THAKROOM!
"THE BIGGER THEY ARE," HUH? WHAT WAS THAT HE SAID ABOUT THE GOD OF WAR--?
ARES... WHOM YOU ONCE KNEW BY HIS ROMAN NAME, MARS.* I THOUGHT ONLY HADES WAS INVOLVED IN THIS ATTACK ON OLYMPUS, BUT I WAS WRONG.
THE GOD OF DEATH HAS AN ALLY IN THE GOD OF WAR.
*AS DID WE, UNTIL RECENT DAYS.--ALAN
I WONDER IF ARES KNOWS HE HAS ANOTHER, HIDDEN ALLY-- THE ANTI-MONITOR?
BUT OF MORE IMPORTANCE-- WHERE ARE THE GODS OF MOUNT OLYMPUS?
ASK HIM, ANGEL. UNLESS I'M WAY OFF BASE...
21

HERE COMES THE AR-GOD NOW, AND E'S BROUGHT A EW FRIENDS.
ARES AND HADES... RIDING IN COMMAND OF AN ARMY OF THE DEAD!
THEY ARE THE SHADES OF LEGEND, WARRIORS WHOSE NAMES ARE HALLOWED IN THE EPICS OF HOMER... MEN WHO FOUGHT WITH FIRE AND FURY, FOR BLOOD AND HONOR AND DESTINY...
AGAMEMNON, LEADER OF THE ACHAEAN GREEKS AT TROY... ACHILLES, FINEST WARRIOR OF AN AGE... ODYSSEUS, BRILLIANT TACTITIAN, FAVORITE OF ATHENA, WANDERER OF ANCIENT SEAS... AJAX, GIANT AMONG MEN, SIMPLE AND LOYAL...
THEY ARE HERE, THEY AND TENS OF THOUSANDS AS NOBLE AND TRUE... RAISED FROM SHADOW TO BATTLE ONCE MORE FOR GODS, AGAINST GODS, IN THE NAME OF HATRED AND AMBITION.
22

AND IF THEY COULD FEEL, THESE SHADOWS THAT ONCE WERE MEN, WHAT WOULD THEY FEEL?
REGRET? RESENTMENT THAT THEIR WELL-EARNED REST HAS BEEN SO RUDELY BROKEN? RAGE?
WE MAY NEVER KNOW, FOR THEIR LONG-DEAD VOICES ARE SILENT, AND THEIR EYES REFLECT ONLY THE DEEP DARKNESS OF THE GRAVE...
AMAZON! I SEE YOU FOUND MY LITTLE ENCHANTMENT LESS THAN AMUSING. NO MATTER.
IN HONOR OF THE BATTLES WE ONCE FOUGHT, I OFFER YOU A SECOND CHANCE TO SURRENDER... OR SUFFER MY GODLY WRATH.
YOUR THREATS DON'T FRIGHTEN ME, ARES. YOU FEE ON WAR, BUT IT'S A FEAST YOU'VE NEVER PREPARED PERSONALLY.
WHERE HAV YOU IMPRISONE YOUR SISTERS AND BROTHER: WHAT HAVE YO DONE TO THE GODS OF MOU OLYMPUS?
'TWAS HADES WHO GAVE ME THE SPELL--AND I DID WITH THEM NO MORE THAN THEY'VE ALREADY DONE TO THEMSELVES.
BLOODLESS AND WITHOUT PASSION HAVE THEY BEEN IN SPIRIT THESE TWO HUNDRED CENTURIES, FORGOTTEN BY MANKIND... REMEMBERED ONLY IN LEGEND.
TIME AND AGAIN THEY IGNORED MY DEMAND FOR WAR AGAINST FAITHLESS HUMANITY. BLOODLESS AND WITHOUT PASSION WERE THEY, IN WORD AND DEED.
BLOODLESS AND WITHOUT PASSION THEY ARE NOW AND WILL FOREVER REMAIN.
FOR HERE, NOW AND EVERMORE, ARES RULES OLYMPUS.
FWOOOSH!

SSSSHHSH
TURNABOUT IS FAIR PLAY.
THANKS, STEVE.
ARE YOU READY?
AS READY AS I'LL EVER BE.
SISTERS AND COUSINS, HOLA! FOR OLYMPUS AND PARADISE ISLAND, STRIKE!
HOLA! FOR OLYMPUS AND PARADISE ISLAND!
HOLA
HOLA!
NO...
24

...TWO ARMIES OF AMAZONS... PINCERING MY FORCES BETWEEN THEM...!
TACTICAL DISASTER! IT CANNOT BE! IT MUST NOT BE!
HOLA! FOR OLYMPUS!
HOLA! FOR ATALANTA!
HOLA!
YOU WERE RIGHT, DIANA. THE MORTAL WARRIORS OF ATALANTA LEFT THEIR RAIN-FOREST HOME MOST WILLINGLY, TO FIGHT BESIDE THEIR SISTER AMAZONS IN THIS TIME OF NEED.
KORE! YOU BROUGHT THEM, AS YOU PROMISED!
THEY, AND YOUR SISTERS FROM PARADISE ISLAND. NOW, AT LAST, THE BREACH BETWEEN MORTAL AND IMMORTAL AMAZON IS HEALED BY HONOR.
FROM THIS HOUR FORTH, THERE IS BUT ONE AMAZON FAMILY... ONE SISTERHOOD... ONE DREAM.
THANK YOU, GODDESS... FOR ALL YOU'VE DONE.
STEVE... STAY WITH KORE. HELP HER FIND THE GODS OF OLYMPUS. NO MATTER WHAT WE DO, ONLY THEY CAN DECIDE THIS BATTLE.
WAIT A MINUTE-- I'M NOT LEAVING YOU, NOT NOW--
DO YOU BELIEVE IN DESTINY, MY DARLING? I DO.

UR TWO LIVES HAVE BEEN
NTWINED BY FATE SINCE
BEFORE THE WORLD WAS
BORN.
WHATEVER HAPPENS... NOW OR IN THE FUTURE...
...WE'LL BE TOGETHER TILL THE END OF TIME.
HOLA!
KORE, YOU'RE A GODDESS...
WHATEVER THAT MEANS.
CAN YOU SEE THE FUTURE?
THIS CRISIS DIANA TOLD ME ABOUT... THIS CONFLICT BETWEEN MONITOR AND ANTI-MONITOR, BETWEEN LIFE AND DEATH, WITH WORLDS AND REALITIES HANGING IN THE BALANCE... DO YOU KNOW HOW IT WILL END?
WILL I EVER SEE HER AGAIN?
YOU LOVE HER, STEVE TREVOR?

MORE THAN LIFE ITSELF. I THINK IT'S THAT LOVE THAT'S BROUGHT ME BACK TO HER, TIME AND AGAIN... EVEN FROM DEATH.
SO, TOO, DID HADES LOVE ME... ONCE. PERHAPS THAT LOVE WILL YET REDEEM US BOTH.
BUT I STILL HAVE TO KNOW, WHAT ABOUT THE--KORE?
IT DOESN'T MATTER. DIANA'S FIGHTING FOR HER LIFE... FOR THE LIVES OF HER SISTERS AND HER GODS... MAYBE FOR A WHOLE UNIVERSE...
...AND I'VE GOT A JOB TO DO!
"AND I MAY JUST HAVE AN IDEA WHERE TO FIND THE GODS OF MOUNT OLYMPUS--!"
HERE IS LEGEND:
DAUGHTER OF HIPPOLYTA, AS LOVELY AS APHRODITE, AS WISE AS ATHENA, WITH THE SPEED OF HERMES AND THE STRENGTH OF HERCULES, SHE IS THE GREATEST OF ALL THE AMAZONS, A BEACON OF LIGHT IN THE GATHERING NIGHT!
UNWISE ARE THOSE WHO FORGET THE POWER SHE WIELDS-- THE POWER OF HOPE, THE POWER OF JUSTICE, THE POWER OF TRUTH RESTORED.
27

GONE! WHAT DID SHE MEAN, HADES' LOVE MIGHT REDEEM THEM BOTH?
SHE IS WONDER WOMAN...
...AND THIS IS HER FINEST HOUR!
28

THAT CURSED WOMAN... THAT AMAZON! SHE WILL BE OUR UNDOING! HER WARRIORS ARE EVERYWHERE... AND BY HER EXAMPLE, SHE INSPIRES THEM TO EVER GREATER HEROISM!
CALM YOURSELF. LOOK MORE CLOSELY.
"YES, OUR SOLDIERS FALL... BUT HAVE YOU FORGOTTEN? OURS IS AN ARMY OF THE DEAD...
"...AND THE DEAD CANNOT DIE BUT ONCE, EVEN AT THE HANDS OF SUCH WARRIORS AS THESE.
"THEY FALL AND RISE AGAIN...
"...AND THOSE THEY SLAY BECOME OUR WARRIORS IN TURN."
WE CANNOT FAIL. THE VICTORY, ARES, IS ALREADY OURS.
YOU'VE ALWAYS BEEN TOO MUCH A DEFEATIST FOR MY TASTE, HADES. I'LL MAKE THE VICTORY CERTAIN BY SLAYING THE AMAZON MYSELF.
AND WHAT WILL YOUR VICTORY WIN YOU, HUSBAND? MORE SOU TO RULE IN HELL?

ORE! REACHEROUS OMAN, WHY YOU COME ME NOW?
I COME TO TURN YOU FROM EVIL, HADES. BUT FIRST SAY WHY YOU SPEAK OF "TREACHERY" TO ME...
...WHO HAS BEEN FAITHFUL TO YOU SINCE TIME BEGAN.
WHERE WAS YOUR FAITH IN THE HOUR OF MY NEED? YOU FLED MY KINGDOM. YOU ABANDONED ME TO UNKNOWN FATE. HE TOLD ME WHY... THE ANTI-MONITOR.
YOU HATE ME. YOU HAVE ALWAYS HATED ME.
USBAND, IT IS YOUR EART THAT IS WISTED BY HATE, NOT MINE.
TRUE, YOU HAVE BEEN MORE A WARDER TO ME THAN A LOVER. YET I HAVE GIVEN YOU FIDELITY AND UNDERSTANDING... MORE THAN THIS...
...I HAVE GIVEN YOU MY LOVE.
IF YOU WILL NOT BELIEVE MY WORDS, THEN BELIEVE THIS, HADES, MY HUSBAND.
AMAZON!
TURN. MEET YOUR DESTINY.
30

I HAD A FEELING IT WOULD COME TO THIS. YOU HATED MY MOTHER, TRICKED HERCULES INTO BETRAYING HER CENTURIES AGO... AND YOU'VE ALWAYS HATED ME.
WHY? BECAUSE I'M A WARRIOR WHO REFUSES TO GLORY IN WAR?
ENOUGH TALK. FIGHT NOW--
--TO THE FINISH!
SKKRAAAAK
ELSEWHERE--
ARES SAID HE'D BEEN GIVEN A SPELL... AND THAT HE USED IT TO DO "WITH THEM NO MORE THAN THEY'VE ALREADY DONE TO THEMSELVES."
"BLOODLESS AND WITHOUT PASSION HAVE THEY BEEN IN SPIRIT THESE TWO CENTURIES, FORGOTTEN BY MANKIND... REMEMBERED ONLY IN LEGEND.
"BLOODLESS AND WITHOU PASSION THEY ARE NOW AND WILL FOREVER REMAIN."

ALL IT A WILD GUESS, BUT VE GOT AN IDEA I KNOW HERE THE GODS ARE. ND I'LL SAY THIS OR ARES.
HE'S GOT A PRETTY FINE TASTE FOR IRONY.
THEY FIGHT, GRUNTING BUT WORDLESS, FOR THERE IS NOTHING LEFT TO SAY.
NEITHER WILL BE SATISFIED WITH LESS THAN TOTAL VICTORY.
FOR THE OTHER, VICTORY MEANS HOPE AND LOVE.
KRASSH!
OR ONE, VICTORY MEANS RUSHING HIS ENEMIES.
AGAINST SUCH POWER, EVEN A GOD MAY NOT LONG PREVAIL...
32

...NOT EVEN A GOD OF DEATH...
HE LIED. THE ANTI-MONITOR LIED. YOU DID NOT FORSAKE ME.
HE IS THE MASTER OF LIES, MY HUSBAND. HE IS DARKNESS. SERVE HIM NO LONGER.
BREAK YOUR PACT WITH ARES. LET THE DEAD HAVE THEIR PEACE.
BUT THE ANTI-MONITOR... HE HOLDS THE UNDERWORLD...
WE WILL FACE HIM TOGETHER, MY LOVE. WHAT WILL BE WILL BE.
"AS YOU SAY, WIFE. OUR DESTINY IS AT HAND."
HIPPOLYTA, DO YOU SEE--? THE DARK WARRIORS FADE LIKE A WAKING DREAM!
I SEE, ATALANTA, BUT I CAN SCARCELY CREDIT MY EYES! WHAT DOES IT MEAN?
IT MEANS, O QUEEN, WE'VE WON... FOR WHATEVER REASON, WHATEVER FATE...
"...WE HAVE WON!"

YOU HEAR, ARES? YOUR ALLY HAS ABANDONED YOU. YOU HAVE NO ARMY, YOU HAVE NO WAR!
IT'S OVER!
I STILL HOLD THE GODS, AMAZON! THEY ARE MY HOSTAGES! NOT EVEN HADES KNOWS WHERE I'VE IMPRISONED THEM--ONLY I HAVE THAT KNOWLEDGE!
YOU HAVE NOTHING, ARES, BUT YOUR OWN BRITTLE HATE!
KRRACK!
HE AXE BREAKS ITH A SOUND IKE A CRACK OF HUNDER, SHATTERING OPES, DREAMS, AND ITTER FANTASIES... ND IT IS ECHOED N INSTANT LATER Y ANOTHER OUND, A CREAK F SLIDING MARBLE, ND A WILD RIUMPHANT ELL...
SHE KNOWS THAT YELL. IT IS THE ONLY WARNING SHE NEEDS.
34

HER DIVE CARRIES HER TO SAFETY.
ARES IS NOT SO QUICK...
...NOR SO FORTUNATE.
ANGEL! I DID IT--I FOUND THEM! ARES HID THEM IN PLAIN SIGHT-- "BLOODLESS AND WITHOUT PASSION"--JUST LIKE HE SAID!
STEVE, PLEASE-- GO SLOWLY! YOU FOUND WHO?
NOT--?
THE GODS OF MOUNT OLYMPUS!
ARES HID THEM INSIDE THEIR OWN MARBLE STATUES! BUT NOW THEY'RE FREE, ANGEL! WE'VE WON!
WOULD THAT IT WERE SO, STEVE TREVOR. YOU HAVE WON A BATTLE, ALL OF YOU... PARTICULARLY YOU, DIANA. BUT THE WAR IS STILL IN DOUBT.
THE ANTI-MONITOR HAS TURNED HIS ATTENTION AWAY FROM OUR AFFAIRS, BUT FOR ONLY A TIME, I FEAR.
BEFORE ANOTHER DAWN, YOU WILL AGA BE CALLED TO BATTL AND WHAT THE OUT-COME OF THAT STRUGGLE MAY BE.. NOT EVEN THE GOD THEMSELVES CAN KNOW.
PERHAPS WE COME AT LAST TO THE FINAL DARKNESS.

STEVE...
...YOU REMEMBER WHAT I SAID TO YOU BEFORE WE LEFT WASHINGTON?
I WANT TO SEAL OUR LOVE. NOW AND FOREVER. IN THE EYES OF THE GODS AND IN THE EYES OF MY AMAZON SISTERS.
EVEN AFTER WHAT ZEUS JUST SAID? WE COULD ALL BE GONE TOMORROW...
HASN'T THAT ALWAYS BEEN TRUE? HAVEN'T WE ALWAYS FACED AN UNCERTAIN FUTURE, EVERY DAY OF OUR LIVES? WHAT'S DIFFERENT ABOUT THIS?
EY, ZEUS...
...HOW ARE YOU AT PERFORMING MARRIAGES?
MOTHER... BE HAPPY FOR ME. I LOVE HIM. AND I LOVE YOU.
NO MORE THAN I LOVE YOU, DAUGHTER. DAUGHTER OF MY HEART, MY ONLY CHILD, MY DEAREST DIANA...
36

THE SKIES ABOVE OLYMPUS ARE CLEAR NOW... AS IF A PASSING STORM HAD PAUSED, RETREATING FOR A TIME BEFORE GATHERING ITS FORCES ANEW.
AND THE DAY IS HUSHED, SAVE FO ONE RICH VOICE, ECHOING WITH DEPTHS OF WISDOM AND POWER UNIMAGINABLE BY MORTAL MAN...

CAN'T SLEEP?
I HAD A DREAM. YOU AND I... AFTER THIS IS OVER... WALKING IN THE SUNLIGHT IN A GOLDEN FIELD. WITH OUR CHILD. ALL OF US TOGETHER. IT WAS A LOVELY DREAM.
"DO YOU BELIEVE IN DESTINY, MY DARLING? I DO.
"OUR TWO LIVES HAVE BEEN ENTWINED BY FATE SINCE BEFORE THE WORLD WAS BORN.
"WHATEVER HAPPENS... NOW OR IN THE FUTURE...
"...WE'LL BE TOGETHER TILL THE END OF TIME."
DEDICATED TO THE MEMORY OF DR. CHARLES MOULTON.
38
NEXT MONTH: IN CRISIS ON INFINITE EARTHS #12--
WONDER WOMAN FACES HER GREATEST, FINAL CHALLENGE! NOTHING WILL EVER BE THE SAME AGAIN--NOTHING!

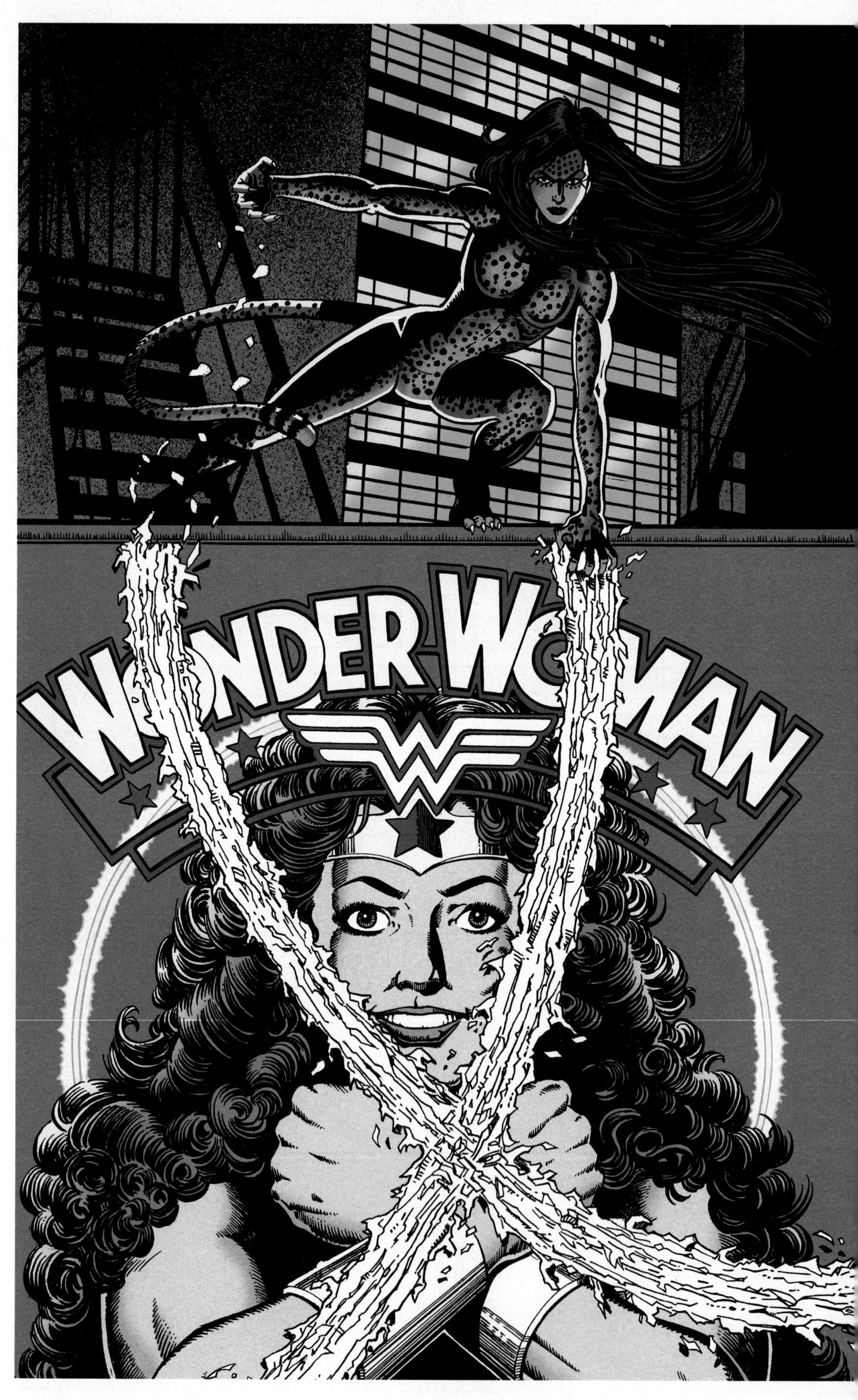

LISTEN! CAN YOU HEAR IT?
ABOVE THE RUMBLE OF THE TRAFFIC AND THE NEON'S CRACKLING HUM?
THERE ARE DRUMS IN THE NIGHT!
AND, TO THE RHYTHM OF THE DRUMS, THERE IS CHANTING!
THE OLD MAN STANDS ON THE BALCONY, HIS WEATHERED FACE AWASH WITH MOONLIGHT--
--AND RAZORED DEATH GLEAMS BRIGHTLY IN HIS HAND!
HE TURNS, AND THE DRUMS GROW LOUDER--
--AS IF KNOWING WHAT IS NEXT TO COME...
MORE OFTEN THAN HE CARES TO REMEMBER, THE OLD MAN HAS PERFORMED THE SACRED RITUAL--
--AND HE PRAYS EACH TIME WILL BE THE LAST!
TONIGHT WAS THE NIGHT OF THE KILL--
--THE NIGHT OF THE HUNGER--
--THE NIGHT WHEN THE DRUMS ARE ONE WITH HER HEART--
--AND HER HEART BEATS QUICK AND STRONG...
TONIGHT IS THE NIGHT OF THE BLOODFEAST!
1

GENTLY, THE OLD MAN TAPES UP HER WOUND...
IN THE MORNING, THERE WILL BE NO SCAR...
SUCH IS THE GOD'S GIFT OF HEALING...
SUCH IS ITS CURSE...
BUT NOW THE GOD GROWS HUNGRY...
NOW MUST THE GOD BE FED...
...THE JEALOUS GOD...
...THE PLANT-GOD...
...THE FRAIL GOD GIVEN LIFE BY THE WOMAN, THAT SHE MIGHT LIVE AS WELL...
TO THE REST OF THE SACRED POTION, THE OLD MAN ADDS THE PRECIOUS BLOOD--
--AND THE DRUMS GROW LOUDER STILL!
DC COMICS
Presents
WONDER WOMAN
BLOOD
OF THE
CHEETAH
Plot and layouts GEORGE PÉREZ
script LEN WEIN
finishes BRUCE D. PATTERSON
letters J. COSTANZA
colors T. WOOD
editor KAREN BERGER
thanks to BOB SMITH
SATED NOW, THE PLANT-GOD SIGHS IN CONTENTMENT--
--AND THE OLD MAN PREPARES TO RETURN HIS MISTRESS--AND ITS SLAVE--TO HER BED...
FOR MOST OF THE APPROACHING DAY, BARBARA MINERVA WILL SLEEP--
--FOR THE ECHO OF THE DRUMS HAS FINALLY CEASED!
2

WAKEFIELD, MASSACHUSETTS, ONE WEEK LATER:
FOR THE PRINCESS DIANA, CHOSEN OF THE AMAZONS, THERE IS STILL NO GREATER EXHILARATION THAN THE SHEER JOY OF FLYING--
--THE INVIGORATING FEELING OF THE BRISK BREEZE WHIPPING WILDLY PAST HER FACE--
--THE INCOMPARABLE SENSATION OF PURE UNBRIDLED FREEDOM!
3

AND FOR PUBLICIST MYNDI MAYER, WATCHING FROM THE WOODS NEARBY, THE THRILL, THOUGH VICARIOUS, IS NO LESS REAL...
THIS IS GOING TO BE SENSATIONAL!
THAT LETTER FROM DR. MINERVA COULDN'T HAVE COME AT A BETTER TIME.
IF SHE REALLY DOES HAVE THE SECOND GIRDLE OF GAEA, IT COULD CHANGE DIANA'S WHOLE PERCEPTION OF HER AMAZON HISTORY--!
AND IT WOULDN'T EXACTLY BE A BAD PUBLICITY COUP EITHER!
YOU'D MERCHANDISE MOTHER TERESA IF YOU COULD MANAGE IT, WOULDN'T YOU?
THE THOUGHT HAS CROSSED MY MIND, PROFESSOR.
HI, MS. MAYER!
HI, YOURSELF, CUTIE.
SORRY IF I SNAPPED AT YOU, MYNDI--
--BUT I'M WORRIED ABOUT DIANA!
WELL, I CAN'T IMAGINE WHY, JULIA!
JUST LOOK AT HER!
"I HAVEN'T SEEN HER THIS HAPPY SINCE I'VE KNOWN HER!
"BARBARA MINERVA'S LETTER WAS LIKE A TONIC!"
IF THE LETTER'S TRUE, ARE YOU GONNA HAVE A PARTY TO CELEBRATE?
CAN I COME?
CAN I BRING A FRIEND?
GOT SOMEBODY SPECIAL IN MIND, SWEET THING?
LET'S JUST SAVE THE CELEBRATION TILL IT'S APPROPRIATE, OKAY?
I'VE DONE A BIT OF CHECKING INTO THIS DR. BARBARA MINERVA'S REPUTATION--
--AND SHE'S ABOUT AS SHADY AS YOUR AVERAGE WEEPING WILLOW!
SO SHE'S NOT A SAINT--! SO WHAT?
YOU AND DIANA HAVE ALREADY DISCUSSED THIS--AND YOU KNOW SHE WANTS TO AT LEAST TALK TO THE LADY.
BESIDES, I'LL BE WITH DIANA FOR THE MEETING WHILE YOU AND VANESSA ARE IN SCHOOL!
"LIKE IT OR NOT, PROFESSOR, DIANA IS A RESPONSIBLE ADULT-
"--AND SHE DOESN'T NEED A SECOND MOTHER!"

MIDTOWN BOSTON, LATER THAT SAME MORNING:
C'MON, HONEY-- RELAX!
HOW CAN I, MYNDI -- WHEN SO MUCH DEPENDS UPON THIS MEETING?
SHE ISN'T GOING TO BITE, YOU KNOW.
I MEAN, WHAT'S THE WORST THAT COULD HAPPEN?
YOU DON'T UNDERSTAND, MYNDI --
IF WHAT BARBARA MINERVA SAYS IS TRUE, IT COULD CHANGE MY ULTIMATE PURPOSE HERE IN MAN'S WORLD --
-- AND AFFECT THE VERY DESTINY OF THE AMAZONS!
OU'RE NOT HELPING MY CASE AT--
DING
ENTHOUSE FLOOR-- WE'RE HERE!
MAY HERA HELP US.
UH... HI.
MYNDI MAYER AND THE PRINCESS DIANA TO SEE DOCTOR MINERVA?
AYE--DE MADAM IS EXPECTING YOU.
PLEASE, CHUMA--BRING OUR GUESTS SOME REFRESHMENT!
I'LL TAKE A KAHLUA AND CREAM.
I AM NOT THIRSTY, THANK YOU.
YOU ARE...?
THE WOMAN WHO WROTE YOU, PRINCESS.
I AM BARBARA MINERVA.
SHALL WE SIT DOWN?
YOU DO UNDERSTAND WE HAVE THINGS TO DISCUSS--PUBLICITY AND PROMOTION-- BEFORE WE GET DOWN TO BUSINESS?!
ALL IN GOOD TIME, MS. MAYER.
I HAVE LOOKED FORWARD TO THIS MEETING, PRINCESS.
DID YOU BRING THE LASSO AS I ASKED?
DIANA?
DO NOT WORRY. IT IS ALWAYS WITH ME--
--AS BEFITS A GIFT FROM THE GODS!
5

YOUR DRINK, MISS.
THANKS MUCHLY, SWEET THING.
I HAVE SHOWN YOU MY LASSO, DOCTOR--FORGED FROM THE GOLDEN GIRDLE OF THE EARTH-GODDESS GAEA HERSELF!
NOW, PLEASE--MAY I SEE YOUR GIRDLE?
IT IS EVERYTHING PROFESSOR KAPATELIS DESCRIBED IN HER ARTICLE -- AND MORE!
ABSOLUTELY BREATH-TAKING!
IF YOU WILL EXCUSE ME FOR A MOMENT, I WILL RETURN WITH THE RELIC I DESCRIBED TO YOU IN MY LETTER!
PLEASE--HURRY!
I ALSO HAVE MUCH DOCUMENTATION TO SHOW YOU--
--EVIDENCE WHICH WILL PROVE THAT--
--THAT--
--NO--
NO--THERE IS--NO DOCUMENTATION--!
THERE IS--NO GIRDLE--!
THERE--IS--NO--BARBA--
RRAAARRGGHH
THIS CURSED LASSO--!
TAKE--TAKE IT AWAY!!
MADAM, ARE YOU ALL RIGHT?
WHAT DO YOU MEAN--THERE IS NO SECOND GIRDLE?
I BELIEVED YOUR LETTER--! I TRUSTED YOU!

WHY WOULD YOU BETRAY ME THIS WAY, DOCTOR? YOU ARE A SISTER?!
I TURNED AWAY FROM JULIA TO MEET YOU!
NO, PLEASE-- WAIT! I ONLY WANTED TO MEET YOU--!
WE HAVE TO TALK--!
SWEET THING-- I'M SORRY!
I THOUGHT SHE WAS LEGIT!
NO, MYNDI-- YOU THOUGHT ONLY OF YOURSELF!
JULIA WAS RIGHT--YOU CARE NOTHING ABOUT ME!
YOU ARE INTERESTED SOLELY IN EXPLOITING ME!
HOW COULD ONE WOMAN DO THAT TO ANOTHER?
DIANA-- PLEASE!
PLEASE WAIT!
< GODDESSES OF OLYMPUS! PRAY GRANT THY WAYWARD DAUGHTER SOME SIGN! >
< HELP ME TO UNDERSTAND THIS MADNESS! >
GREAT.
JUST FREAKING FABULOUS!
NOW WHAT?
BUT QUESTIONS ARE ALL MYNDI MAYER HAS LEFT...
THE ANSWERS ARE ALREADY LONG GONE!
7

THE KAPATELIS SUMMER HOME, LATER THAT SAME AFTERNOON:
YEAH... UH-HUH... I UNDERSTAND...
I'LL TELL HER, MIZ MAYER.
SHE WON'T LISTEN--BUT I'LL TELL HER.
BUT SHE HAS TO LISTEN, SWEET THING!
SHE HAS TO LET ME APOLOGIZE!
WE'VE GOT TOUR DATES TO TALK ABOUT-- A CAMPAIGN TO RUN!
SHE CAN'T JUST CUT ME OFF LIKE THIS!
WELL, NOW ISN'T REALLY THE BEST TIME TO TALK TO DIANA, MIZ MAYER.
MOM IS STILL OUTSIDE WITH HER, TRYIN' TO CALM HER DOWN!
I'LL LET YOU KNOW HOW IT GOES. YEAH... BYE.
SO MUCH HAS HAPPENED SINCE WE BEGAN THIS WONDER WOMAN TOUR, JULIA-- SO MUCH HAS CHANGED!
I HAVE SO MANY QUESTIONS... I FEEL SO LOST...
WILL I LEAVE MAN'S WORLD HAVING TAUGHT PEOPLE NOTHING MORE THAN MY NAME?
EVERYTHING SEEMED SO SIMPLE ON PARADISE ISLAND-- YET NOW I REALIZE I AM NO LONGER LIKE MY SISTER AMAZONS!
MY LIFE IS PART OF SOME GREATER DESIGN -- AND STOPPING ARES WAS BUT ONE SMALL PART OF IT!
MY NAME... MY COSTUME ...MY MISSION...
THEY ARE ALL TATTERS OF SOME VAST TAPESTRY-- LACKING THE THREAD TO MAKE THEM WHOLE!
DIANA, DON'T-- YOU'VE ACCOMPLISHED MUCH IN YOUR TIME HERE!
AND TIME IS SOMETHING THIS OLD WORLD NEEDS-- TO LEARN FROM YOU!
UNFORTUNATELY, JULIA--
-- TIME IS THE ONE COMMODITY I CANNOT AFFORD TO SPARE!

THE RENTED PENTHOUSE OF BARBARA MINERVA, THAT SAME NIGHT:
--DELICATELY PLUCKING THE RIPENED BERRIES FROM THE GOD-PLANT, AND CRUSHING THEM TO PASTE--
IN THE RITUAL CHAMBER, THE OLD MAN NAMED CHUMA PREPARES THE SACRED ELIXIR--
--ALL THE WHILE CHANTING, AS IF TO THE SOUND OF DISTANT DRUMS!
IN HER PRIVATE QUARTERS, BARBARA MINERVA READIES HER-SELF FOR THE ORDEAL YET TO COME--
--PAINTING HER FACE IN THE ANCIENT MANNER--
--PREPARING HERSELF FOR WAR!
DID YOU SEE HOW THE LASSO WORKED, CHUMA? HOW IT FORCED ME TO SPEAK THE TRUTH?
IT IS EVERYTHING I COULD HAVE HOPED FOR! IT MUST BE MINE!
IS THE ELIXIR READY, OLD MAN?
AYE, MA'AM.
YOU MUST DRINK IT NOW--
--RAW--
--WHILE DE BREW STILL BURNS!
IT SMELLS LIKE FIRE, OLD MAN!
IT SMELLS LIKE--LIFE!

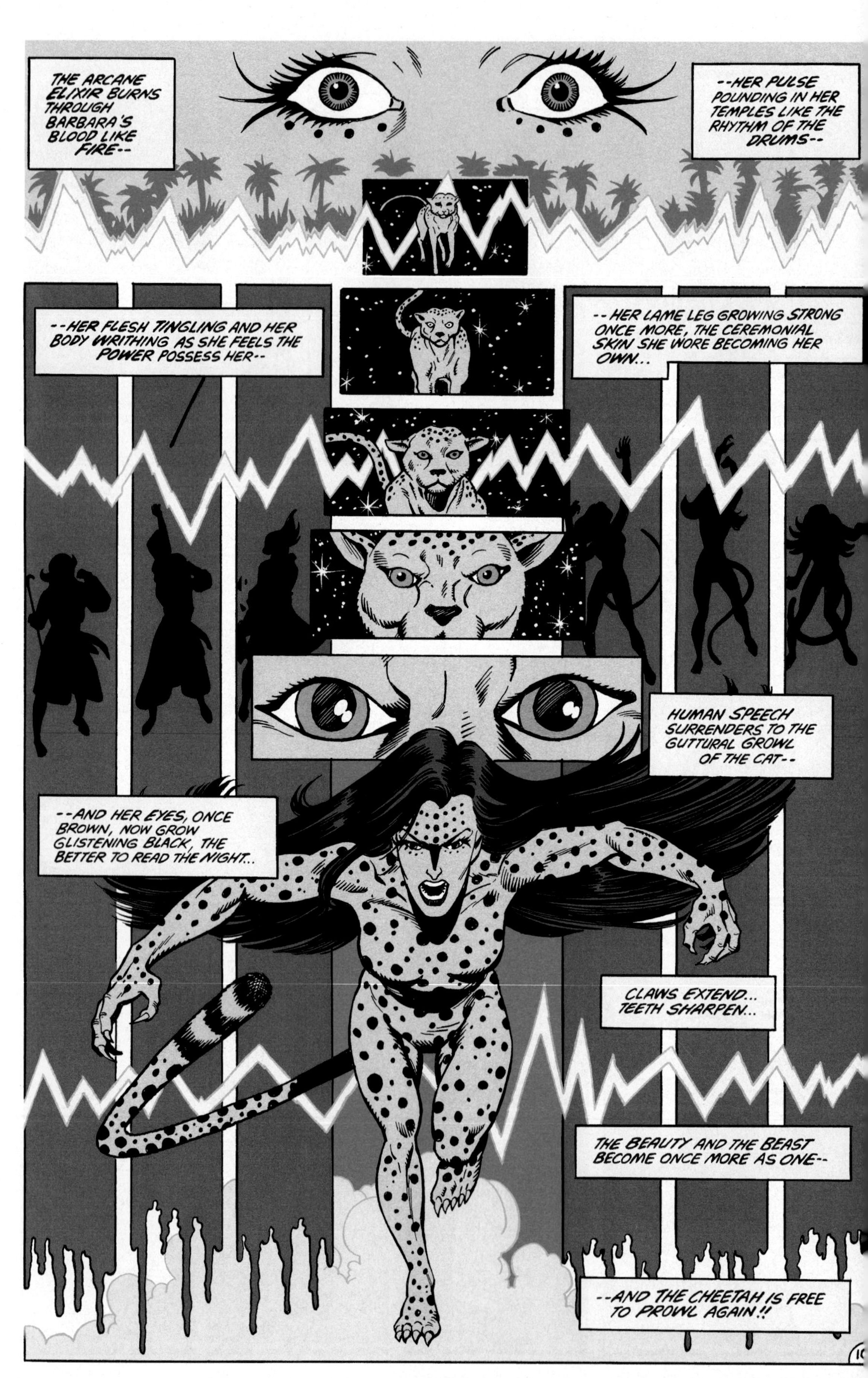
THE ARCANE ELIXIR BURNS THROUGH BARBARA'S BLOOD LIKE FIRE--
--HER PULSE POUNDING IN HER TEMPLES LIKE THE RHYTHM OF THE DRUMS--
--HER FLESH TINGLING AND HER BODY WRITHING AS SHE FEELS THE POWER POSSESS HER--
--HER LAME LEG GROWING STRONG ONCE MORE, THE CEREMONIAL SKIN SHE WORE BECOMING HER OWN...
HUMAN SPEECH SURRENDERS TO THE GUTTURAL GROWL OF THE CAT--
--AND HER EYES, ONCE BROWN, NOW GROW GLISTENING BLACK, THE BETTER TO READ THE NIGHT...
CLAWS EXTEND... TEETH SHARPEN...
THE BEAUTY AND THE BEAST BECOME ONCE MORE AS ONE--
--AND THE CHEETAH IS FREE TO PROWL AGAIN!!

HER CLAWS GOUGING HAND-HOLDS IN THE BUILDING'S SHEER FACE, THE CHEETAH DESCENDS INTO THE DARKNESS--
--INTO THE CONCRETE JUNGLE THAT IS HER HUNT-ING GROUND--
LEAVING THE OLD MAN BEHIND TO WAIT--
--AND TO PONDER...
SHE BE THE LAST OF HER KIND, DAT ONE--
--AS HER GOD BE DE LAST OF ITS KIND--
--YET HER SURVIVAL BE IN DE HANDS OF A FICKLE GOD INDEED!
TANK YOU, ANCIENT ONE, FOR BRINGING DE CHEETAH BACK TO ME!
I PRAY YOU-- KEEP HER SAFE!
AND IN THE DARKNESS, THE CHEETAH STALKS THROUGH THE SHADOWS OF BOSTON--
--DRAWN BY SCENT AND INSTINCT UNERRINGLY TO HER PREY!
LISTEN! CAN YOU HEAR IT?
THERE ARE DRUMS IN THE NIGHT!
THE LONG HUNT HAS BEGUN...
BRINNNG
BRINNNG
HELLO? LT. ETTA CANDY SPEAKING.
STEVE? STEVE TREVOR?
WHO--?
OH, COLONEL --IT'S SO GOOD TO HEAR YOUR VOICE!
...AND THE INVESTIGATION CONTINUES INTO THE MYSTERIOUS DEATH OF LOCAL CRIMINAL TAMSYN McCONNELL...
ANIMAL ATTACK
...WHO WAS SLAIN LAST WEEK, APPARENTLY BY SOME WILD ANIMAL...

ETTA, I'M AFRAID I WON'T BE COMING BACK TO BOSTON TOMORROW AS INTENDED.
JUST GOT A LETTER FROM HOME AND I HAVE TO RETURN TO OKLAHOMA AS QUICKLY AS POSSIBLE...
...MY FATHER IS DYING.
OH, STEVE...I'M SO SORRY. LOOK, I'VE GOT SOME LEAVE TIME COMING.
AND YOU SOUND LIKE YOU COULD USE SOME COMPANY.
THAT'S GREAT, ETTA--I APPRECIATE THE OFFER.
LET ME CHECK WITH MY AUNT EDNA AND WORK OUT THE ARRANGEMENTS.
GOD, IT FEELS STRANGE TO BE GOING HOME AGAIN.
SO MUCH HAS CHANGED SINCE I WAS A KID!
THE OUTSKIRTS OF BOSTON, SEVERAL MINUTES LATER:
SHE MOVES THROUGH THE NIGHT AS THOUGH PART OF IT--
--COVERING GROUND WITH ALMOST SUPERHUMAN SPEED--
--NOSTRILS FLARED AND SEARCHING--
--KNOWING HER PREY IS SOMEWHERE NEAR--
--ALMOST NEAR ENOUGH NOW TO TASTE...
ABRASIVE TONGUE LICKING LEATHERY LIPS, THE CHEETAH RACES ON--
--FEELING HER HUNGER GROWING, KNOWING IT MUST BE APPEASED...
SOON IT WILL BE TIME FOR THE BLOODFEAST!
12

THE KAPATELIS SUMMER HOME, SEVERAL MINUTES LATER:
DIANA?
DIANA, YOU HERE?
MOM, HAVE YOU SEEN DIANA AROUND?
I THINK SHE'S STILL OUT IN THE WOODS, HONEY.
SO LATE?
IS SHE OKAY?
SHE OFTEN STAYS OUT THERE, BABY -- TO COMMUNE WITH NATURE!
CONSIDERING WHAT A DISASTER TODAY TURNED OUT TO BE --
-- I THINK SHE NEEDS ALL THE MEDITATION TIME SHE CAN GET!
TRUST ME -- SHE'LL COME BACK IN WHEN SHE'S READY.
BESIDES, THAT'S ONE WOMAN WHO CAN TAKE CARE OF HER --
RRRRRR
-- EH?
MOMMY...
...WH-WHAT WAS THAT?
I'M NOT SURE, BABY...
...SOUNDED LIKE IT MIGHT HAVE BEEN SOME SORT OF ANIMAL!
"BUT WHATEVER, I'M SURE IT'S NOTHING TO WORRY ABOUT!"
BY THE SHORE OF THE LAKE, THE AMAZON SLUMBERS, ALONE SAVE FOR A DARING RACCOON WHO HAS SHUFFLED CLOSE TO SHARE HER WARMTH...
13

NOW, IN THE TANGLED BRUSH ABOVE HER, SOMETHING STIRS--
-- SOMETHING SILENT AS THE MOONLIGHT YET QUICK AS A TWITCH--
--SOMETHING THAT CROUCHES UNMOVING, STUDYING ITS PREY--
--OBSERVING THE STEADY RISE AND FALL OF HER CHEST, LISTENING TO THE EVEN RHYTHM OF HER HEARTBEAT--
--DARK EYES NARROWED AS IT SEARCHES FOR THE SLEEPING PREY'S PULSE--
--ANTICIPATING THE WARM GUSH OF BLOOD WHEN RAZORED CLAWS SLASH TENDER FLESH...
THE HUNTER TENSES, SLEEK MUSCLES BUNCHED BENEATH ITS FUR--
--PREPARING ITSELF FOR THE MOMENT--
EH?
--THE EXULTANT MOMENT WHEN IT FINALLY STRIKES!!
WHAT IN--
UURRKK!!
14

THIS ONE IS STRONG, THE HUNTER SENSES INSTANTLY, STRONGER BY FAR THAN THE REST--
--AND THUS THE PREY MUST BE FINISHED SWIFTLY--
--BEFORE IT CAN RALLY ITS RESOURCES TO STRIKE BACK!
WH-WHAT STRUCK ME--?
SEEMED LIKE SOME GREAT CAT--
LIKE A CHEETAH OR AN--
RRRAAPRRR
--AARRGHH!!
THOSE CLAWS-- SO SHARP--!
GREAT HERMES, GRANT ME SPEED--
--OR HER NEXT BLOW MAY SLAY ME!
BLOOD--?!?
BY THE GODS, SHE ACTUALLY DREW BLOOD!
WHAT MANNER OF MONSTER IS SHE?
15

WHATEVER THE REASON FOR HER UNWARRANTED ATTACK--
-- IT IS TIME FOR THE HUNTER TO BECOME THE HUNTED--!
STILL, SHE CANNOT LONG ELUDE ONE WHO POSSESSES THE GOD-GIVEN POWER OF FLIGHT!
UUNNHH!!
RRRAARRR
IMPOSSIBLE! NOTHING HUMAN CAN MOVE SO SWIFTLY--!
SHE CONTINUES TO ATTACK WHEN ANY SANER MIND WOULD FLEE!
THIS CHEETAH IS CONSTANT AGGRESSION IN HUMAN FORM--
--AND SHE HAS CHOSEN ME AS HER TARGET!
HER CLAWS WILL SCRATCH OUT MY EYES IF THEY REACH ME--!
HER FANGS WILL RIP OUT MY THROAT--!
SHE WILL QUICKLY TEAR ME TO PIECES--
--UNLESS I STRIKE BACK NOW--
--AND STRIKE HARD!!
16

FOR AN INSTANT, THE SHE-BEAST HOLDS HER GROUND, CROUCHES ONCE MORE TO SPRING--
--AND THEN, AS IF SUDDENLY THINKING BETTER OF IT, SHE HURLS HERSELF INTO THE BUSH...
SHE'S STILL CLOSE AT HAND, STALKING ME--!
I CAN FEEL IT--!
YET STILL AM I THE SPIRITUAL DAUGHTER OF THE GODDESS ARTEMIS!
MINE ARE THE HEIGHTENED INSTINCTS OF THE HUNTRESS!
MUST CONCENTRATE--
--INCREASE MY STATE OF AWARENESS--!
LISTEN, DIANA...
HEAR YOUR OWN HEART-BEAT...
RECOG-NIZE ITS RHYTHMS...
NOW SEARCH THE BRUSH FOR A SECOND PULSE...
FIND THE HEAVING HEART OF THE BEAST...
THERE!
RRRAARRGH??
THE HUNT IS ENDED, CHEETAH!
YOU ARE MINE!!
17

BOUND BY THE GLEAMING GOLDEN LARIAT, THE CHEETAH SUDDENLY HESITATES--
--AS IF AT LAST SUCCUMBING TO THE LASSO'S AWESOME ARCANE POWER--
--BUT THEN, IMPOSSIBLY...
GREAT HERA! THE LASSO HAS NO EFFECT ON HER!
THE SHE-BEAST IS PULLING ME TOWARD HER--!
DIGGING IN HER HEELS, THE PRINCESS DIANA HOLDS HER OWN GROUND--
--AND THE STRAIN OF THE RESULTANT STALEMATE CAN QUICKLY BE SEEN ON THE TORTURED FACES OF THE TWO COMBATANTS...
THE CHEETAH HISSES IN INARTICULATE RAGE, SPITTLE FLYING FROM HER LEATHERY LIPS IN A FINE SPRAY--
--WHILE THE AMAZON MERELY CLENCHES HER TEETH IN GRIM DETERMINATION, ATTEMPTING TO STUDY THE FACE OF HER FOE--
--AND THUS GIVING THE SHE-BEAST THE INFINITESIMAL OPENING SHE NEEDS...
UUNNHH!!
RRAARR
FALLEN TREE TRUNK HAS ME PINNED--!
CAN'T MOVE--!
THE CHEETAH HAS WON!
18

BLAM!
NO!
NO!!
JULIA, WHY--?
SHE WAS GOING TO KILL YOU, DIANA.
I HAD NO OTHER CHOICE!
WAIT! IF SHE IS STILL BOUND BY MY LASSO--!
PERHAPS I CAN PULL HER UP BEFORE SHE--
--SLIPS--
--FREE--
DIANA-- WAIT--!
NO TIME--!
SHE MAY STILL BE ALIVE DOWN THERE!
THE WATERS, SO DARK--
--AND THE CURRENTS HERE, SO SWIFT--!
NO USE--!
THERE IS NO WAY I CAN FIND HER!
19

MOM, WHAT'S HAPPENING OUT HERE? I HEARD THE SHOT AND--!
HEY--WHERE'S DIANA?
VANESSA, I THOUGHT I TOLD YOU TO STAY HOME!
WHILE THERE'S TROUBLE OUT HERE?!
NO WAY, JOSE!
: GASP :
DIANA, IS SHE--?
I COULD FIND NO TRACE OF THE SHE-BEAST IN THAT EBONY DEEP, JULIA.
WHATEVER SHE WAS... WHATEVER SHE WANTED FROM ME...
THE CHEETAH IS--
--GONE--
LISTEN! CAN YOU HEAR IT?
THE SUDDEN, ALL-OPPRESSIVE SILENCE?
THE SOUND OF THE DRUMMING HAS FINALLY STOPPED!
THE HEART OF BOSTON:
SEVERAL DAYS LATER...
MYNDI MAYER SPEAKING!
IT'S YOUR QUARTER, SWEET THING--DON'T WASTE IT!
OH--IT'S ONLY YOU, CHRISSIE. SOME PROBLEM AT THE OFFICE?
WORST KIND, MIZ MAYER. I JUST GOT A MESSAGE FROM JULIA KAPATELIS--!
EVEN AS WE SPEAK, YOUR PRINCESS DIANA IS HEADING HOME!
SHE'S WHAT-?!?
BUT WHAT ABOUT ALL MY PUBLICITY PLANS?!
WE'VE GOT A CONTRACT, BLAST IT!
SHE CAN'T DO THIS TO ME!!
20

GAYHEAD CLIFFS, MARTHA'S VINEYARD:
IT SEEMS SOMEHOW FITTING THAT I SHOULD DEPART FROM MAN'S WORLD AT THIS PARTICULAR PLACE...
THESE CLIFFS ARE SO LIKE THOSE OF MY BELOVED PARADISE ISLAND.
ONE CAN TRULY BE AT PEACE HERE.
AND YET, DESPITE MY GREAT NEED TO BE AMONG MY OWN AGAIN, I CANNOT HELP REGRETTING THAT I MUST LEAVE.
TRULY, THIS HAS BECOME A SECOND HOME TO ME...
THEN STAY, DIANA-- PLEASE DON'T GO!
YOU'RE LIKE THE BIG SISTER I NEVER HAD BEFORE!
WHAT'LL I DO WITHOUT YOU?
YOU WILL WATCH OVER YOUR MOTHER, LITTLE ONE-- AND YOU WILL BE STRONG!
BUT I TOO HAVE A MOTHER THAT I LOVE-- AND THE TIME HAS COME TO RETURN TO HER.
I WILL MISS YOU, VANESSA--
--FOR YOU HAVE SHOWN ME A YOUNG WORLD FULL OF BRIGHT PROMISE!
REMEMBER YOUR POWER, LITTLE SISTER--
--AND KNOW I WILL ALWAYS LOVE YOU.
OH, DIANA--!
21

WELL, GUESS THERE'S NO PUTTING THIS OFF ANY LONGER.
YOU TAKE GOOD CARE OF YOURSELF, KIDDO.
JULIA, WHEN THE GODS FIRST LED ME TO YOU, I DID NOT UNDERSTAND WHY--
--BUT NOW I KNOW THEIR STRENGTH AND WISDOM IS WITHIN YOU TOO!
YOU HAVE MADE MY TIME HERE SO MUCH MORE MEANINGFUL...
ALL THAT I HAVE BECOME, I OWE TO YOU.
PLEASE, COULD YOU REMOVE YOUR GLASSES--SO THAT I MAY GAZE INTO YOUR EYES ONE LAST TIME?
FOR YOU, HONEY-- ANYTHING!
HOPE YOU DON'T MIND IF THEY'RE A LITTLE RED, THOUGH...
I'M REALLY GOING TO MISS YOU, DIANA.
I LOVE YOU, JULIA.
KNOWING YOU HAS BEEN ONE OF THIS LIFE'S GREAT JOYS!
AND I YOU, CHILD!
HERE! THIS BAG HAS SOME SOUVENIRS WE THOUGHT YOU MIGHT LIKE... SOME OF YOUR NEWSPAPER CLIPPINGS...
...A PHOTO OF VANESSA AND ME...
THANK YOU, JULIA --I WILL TREASURE THEM.
AND NOW, I FEAR, THE TIME HAS COME FOR ME TO GO!
MAY THE BLESSINGS OF THE GODS BE ALWAYS UPON YOU, MY FRIENDS!
WHATEVER THE FICKLE FATES MAY HAVE IN STORE FOR ME, I AM NOW STRONG ENOUGH TO FACE THEM--
--THANKS TO YOU!
UNTIL WE MEET AGAIN!
SURE...
...UNTIL WE MEET AGAIN...
THEN, BORNE SKYWARD BY THE ENCHANTED SANDALS OF THE FLEET GOD HERMES--
--THE AMAZON PRINCESS IS SWALLOWED BY THE CLOUDS--
--AND VANISHES FROM THE SIGHT OF MAN--
--PERHAPS FOREVER!

RICHARD FRIEND

DIANA, I...
I NEED TO GO.

FIVE DAYS LATER
CENTRAL PARK.
PLEASE, BARBARA, LET ME SAVE YOU FROM THIS CURSE.
LET ME FREE YOU FROM THE CHEETAH!
THE SECRET OF THE CHEETAH
PART ONE
WRITER GEOFF JOHNS PENCILLER TONY S. DANIEL INKERS RICHARD FRIEND & BAT

COLORS TOMEU MOREY LETTERS PATRICK BROSSEAU COVER DANIEL, FRIEND AND MOREY
ASSISTANT EDITOR KATIE KUBERT EDITOR BRIAN CUNNINGHAM

YOU THINK I WANT TO GO BACK TO BEING A PART OF THE HUMANITY YOU FIND SO WONDERFUL?
I DON'T BELIEVE IN HUMANITY!
PEOPLE ARE ANIMALS!
ANIMALS THAT FOOL THEMSELVES INTO THINKING THEY'RE SOMETHING MORE.

THAT'S NOT TRUE, BARBARA. YOU KNOW IT'S NOT.
YOU ARE AS NAIVE AS THE DAY WE MET.
COME NOW, DIANA.
EVEN IF YOUR LASSO DID WORK ON ME, IT WOULDN'T CHANGE WHAT I'M SAYING.
USE YOUR LASSO ON YOUR PRECIOUS FLOCK AND ASK THEM ABOUT THEIR DARKEST DESIRES.
SEE IF YOUR ADORABLE HEART CAN STOMACH WHAT PERVERSIONS YOU EXPOSE WITHIN THEM.
CIVILIZATION IS JUST A MASK THEY ALL WEAR.

I DON'T WANT TO HURT YOU, BARBARA, BUT IF KNOCKING YOU OUT AND DRAGGING YOU HOME IS THE ONLY WAY TO BRING YOU BACK, I'LL DO IT.
KRRKAATCH
OF COURSE YOU WILL.
YOU GREW UP SURROUNDED BY VIOLENCE.
AND YOU'RE STILL DRAWN TO IT.
AAH--

THE TRUTH IS: HUMANITY ARE NOT SHEEP TO SHEPHERD.
THEY ARE CATTLE TO SLAUGHTER.
THE SOONER YOU REALIZE THAT, THE SOONER WE CAN BE FRIENDS AGAIN.
HERE SHE IS!
NO...
WONDER WOMAN?
WHERE DID SHE GO? I HAVE TO FIND HER.
I HAVE TO FIND BARBARA!

"I CAN'T FAIL HER AGAIN."
WASHINGTON, D.C.
MEDICAL CARE UNIT OF A.R.G.U.S.
I'M SURPRISED THEY LET YOU IN HERE.
THEY DIDN'T.
SO, BATMAN, IF THE PENTAGON SEES YOU ON THE SECURITY CAMERAS, THEY CAN ADD BREAKING AND ENTERING TO THEIR GROWING LIST OF RIDICULOUS COMPLAINTS.
THE CAMERAS WON'T SHOW THEM ANYTHING, TREVOR.
CYBORG?
WE NEED SOME INFORMATION ON THE CHEETAH, COLONEL.
WHY? IS DIANA OKAY?
I'M FINE.
THE WATCHTOWER SATELLITE.
HEADQUARTERS OF THE JUSTICE LEAGUE.
WE KNOW YOU'RE FINE. WE'VE JUST NEVER SEEN YOU, UH, KNOCKED DOWN BEFORE.
WONDER WOMAN WAS OBVIOUSLY HOLDING BACK, FLASH.
WHY HOLD BACK?
"BECAUSE BARBARA MINERVA WAS THE FIRST FRIEND DIANA MADE."

THEY MET AT THE SMITHSONIAN, WHERE BARBARA WAS WORKING. HERE WAS A TERRORIST ATTACK, HICH ENDED BEING A COVER-UP TO CONCEAL A ROBBERY.
DIANA CHARGED IN AND DID WHAT SHE DOES BEST.
FOR THE NEXT SEVERAL MONTHS, BARBARA HELPED DIANA AND ME ON CASES THAT TIED TO THE *MYTHOLOGICAL WORLD.*
BUT AFTER WORKING WITH ME, AFTER BEING THERE FOR ME IN SO MANY WAYS, BARBARA'S LIFE WAS DESTROYED.
EVERYONE KNEW BARBARA WAS WORKING WITH WONDER WOMAN, SO SHE BECAME THE GO-TO-PERSON FOR IDENTIFYING AND CATALOGING POTENTIALLY DANGEROUS ARTIFACTS.
SHE OVERSAW ***THE BLACK ROOM*** AT A.R.G.U.S. WHERE WE SORT AND STORE THOSE TYPES OF ITEMS.
ONE DAY, DIANA CAME INTO POSSESSION OF A ***RITUAL DAGGER*** FROM A LOST TRIBE IN THE AMAZON.
BARBARA CUT HERSELF ON IT. AND SHE WAS ***POSSESSED*** BY THE ***GODDESS OF THE HUNT.***
THE BLOODTHIRSTY ***CHEETAH!***
THEY'VE CLASHED ON-AND-OFF FOR YEARS, BUT THE CHEETAH'S ALWAYS BEEN ELUSIVE. SHE DISAPPEARS FOR MONTHS AT A TIME.
"DIANA BLAMES HERSELF FOR WHAT HAPPENED TO BARBARA.
"JUST LIKE SHE'S BLAMING HERSELF FOR ***DAVID GRAVES*** PUTTING ME IN THE HOSPITAL."

I APPRECIATE YOUR LOOKING OUT FOR ME, BUT THIS ISN'T WHY THE JUSTICE LEAGUE EXISTS.
THE CHEETAH IS MY PROBLEM, NOT YOURS.
CAN YOU EXCUSE US FOR A MINUTE? FLASH? CYBORG?
...SURE.
WE'LL BE RIGHT OUTSIDE, UM, WAITING, I GUESS.
LET US HELP YOU FIND YOUR FRIEND.
I DON'T GET INVOLVED WHEN LEX LUTHOR OR METALLO IS CAUSING TROUBLE, DO I?
NOT BECAUSE YOU NEED IT, DIANA, BUT BECAUSE WE WANT TO.
I WANT TO.
IF THIS IS THAT IMPORTANT TO YOU, IF IT INVOLVES HELPING SOMEONE YOU CARE ABOUT, I WANT TO HELP.

WHAT HAPPENED A FEW DAYS AGO, SUPERMAN. IT JUST HAPPENED.
I KNOW. IT WAS A KISS, NOT A COMMITMENT.
BUT IT WAS NICE, DIANA.
IT WAS.

IS IT JUST ME OR IS THIS WEIRD? CYBORG? *VIC?*
HEY, ARE YOU *LISTENING* TO THEM?
I'M TRYING *NOT* TO.
YOU OKAY?
I MEAN *I'M* NOT OKAY. GREEN LANTERN QUIT. BATMAN AND AQUAMAN ARE ARGUING ABOUT WHO'S LEADING THE TEAM. NOW SOMETHING'S GOING ON WITH WONDER WOMAN AND SUPERMAN?
YOU THINK HE'S STILL MAD SHE KICKED HIM INTO THE SIDE OF A CAR?
IF THE LEAGUE GOES AWAY, I DON'T KNOW WHAT I'LL DO. YOU HAVE LIVES YOU CAN GO BACK TO. I DON'T.
WHAT ARE YOU TALKING ABOUT?
IF I'M NOT OUT DEALING WITH THINGS THAT NEED TO BE DEALT WITH, I'M HERE.
YOU STAY *HERE?* BY YOURSELF?
WHEN I'M NOT AT S.T.A.R. LABS GETTING UPGRADE I USUALLY SORT THROUGH INCOMIN DATA. I READ. WATC MOVIES. OCCASIONAL BATMAN NEEDS SOMETHING.
WHERE DO YOU RELAX? WHERE DO YOU SLEEP?
I DON'T NEED TO SLEEP.
SOMETIMES I THINK I AM JUST A *MACHINE* THAT BELIEVES IT'S A KID NAMED *VICTOR STONE.*

C'MON, VIC, THAT WAS JUST ONE OF GRAVES' EVIL SPIRITS TRYING TO GET TO YOU. THEY WERE MESSING WITH ALL OF US.
THAT SPIRIT DIDN'T JUST COME UP WITH IT, FLASH. IT SAID WHAT IT SAID BECAUSE DEEP DOWN I'VE THOUGHT ABOUT IT. HALF OF MY BODY IS GONE. PART OF MY BRAIN IS A COMPUTER.
YOU'RE NOT A ROBOT, VIC. ROBOTS DON'T LAUGH AT JOKES OR TALK ABOUT THEIR FAVORITE TELEVISION SHOWS OR WORRY THAT THEY'RE ROBOTS.
DO YOU EVER FANTASIZE ABOUT MAKING OUT WITH A TOASTER?
NO.
I REST MY CASE.
YOU'RE A FUNNY GUY, FLASH.
C'MON. START CALLING ME BARRY.
NOW WHAT ARE THOSE TWO TALKING ABOUT?

YOU AND I HAVE OTHER RESPONSIBILITIES WE NEED TO FOCUS ON.
LIKE THE CHEETAH?
WE CAN HELP YOU FIND HER.
IT'S NOT THE CHEETAH I NEED TO FIND. IT'S THE LOST TRIBE CONNECTED TO HER.
THEY HAVE TO KNOW MORE ABOUT THE DAGGER THAT TRANSFORMED BARBARA INTO THAT MONSTER. MAYBE THEY CAN HELP.
BUT YOU CAN'T LOCATE THEM?
I HAVEN'T YET.
THEN WE CAN HELP WITH THAT. CYBORG?
I HEARD YOU, SUPERMAN.
HEARD WHAT?
I'M ALREADY SEARCHING AND MAPPING KNOWN AREAS TO COVER OFF WHERE WE DON'T NEED TO LOOK.
I'LL NARROW DOWN THE HUNT BASED ON THE RITUAL DAGGER'S LAST KNOWN LOCATION.
THEN WHEN WE BOOM DOWN I COULD DO SOME RECON. THE TERRAIN MIGHT MAKE IT A LITTLE SLOW, BUT IT SHOULDN'T TAKE ME MORE THAN AN HOUR OR TWO.
YOU DON'T NEED TO DO THIS.
IT'S NO PROBLEM.
HAPPY TO HELP.

THANKS FOR THE INFORMATION, TREVOR.
WHERE ARE YOU GOING?
CYBORG, CAN YOU PICK US UP? TIME TO REGROUP.
WE'RE ON OUR WAY, AND WE'VE GOT A PROPOSED PLAN.
GOOD.
MAYBE I SHOULD TALK TO DIANA. THE WAY WE LEFT THINGS...
WE'LL PASS ON THE MESSAGE.
THANKS.

THE CONGO.
STEVE'S CLEARLY UNHAPPY BEING SHUT OUT LIKE THIS.
BETTER UPSET THAN IN HARM'S WAY AGAIN.
ARE YOU SURE REMOVING HIM AS OUR LIAISON IS THE RIGHT THING FOR THE TEAM? OR HIM?
OR YOU?
WHAT DID YOU FIND, FLASH?
NOT MUCH. THOUGH, TO BE HONEST, THIS ISN'T EXACTLY THE EASIEST AREA TO EXPLORE.
ARE YOU SURE THIS TRIBE LIVES ABOVE GROUND?
THERE'S NOT MUCH I'VE LEARNED ABOUT THEM. EVEN THEIR NAME IS UNKNOWN.
ARE YOU SURE THEY EXIST?
WHAT ARE YOU DOING, SUPERMAN?

LISTENING.
DO YOU HEAR THAT, CYBORG?
I DO. SOME KIND OF CHANTING. ACROSS THE GORGE.
BUT MOVEMENT *BEHIND* US.

IT'S--!
RRROOWWW!
NNGG!
CHEETAH! I GOT--
AAHH!
RRAOWW!

VVMMMMM
SUPERMAN!
YOU'VE BROUGHT YOUR FRIENDS TO THE WRONG PART OF THE WORLD, DIANA.
MY WORLD.
SSSS!
AAH!
SUPERMAN?!
RRRR...

RRROOWWRRR!
NEXT:
THE TRUT
BEHIND TH
CHEETAH

TONY
DANIEL
2012
RICHARD FRIEND

HIDDEN IN THE CONGO.
"<EVERY PEOPLE HAVE THEIR PROTECTORS.>
"<THEY ARE THANKFUL FOR THE GODLIKE BEINGS THAT RISE UP TO WATCH OVER THEM.>
SUPERMAN, STOP!
BOOOMM
<DEITIES WITH GREAT POWER WHO BATTLE AGAINST THE EVILS OF THIS WORLD.>
LET SUPERMAN GO, CHEETAH!
RRRRAOWN
"<THE CHEETAH WAS OUR PROTECTOR.>
RRRR
"<THE CHEETAH WAS OUR SAVIOR.>"
THUNK

<UNTIL BARBARA MINERVA *RUINED* IT ALL.>
<SHE MUST *DIE* SO THAT THE CHEETAH CAN BE *SAVED.*>


# THE SECRET OF THE CHEETAH

CHAPTE TWO

GEOFF JOHNS-WRITER - TONY S. DANIEL-PENCILLE
MATT BANNING & SANDU FLOREA-INKERS - TOMEU MOREY-COLORIST
DAVE SHARPE-LETTERER - TONY S. DANIEL, RICHARD FRIEND AND TOMEU MOREY-COU
KATIE KUBERT-ASST. EDITOR - BRIAN CUNNINGHAM-EDITOR

RRRAAOOWW!
RRRRAAA!
I'LL BE BACK, HARA!
AND NOTHING, NOT EVEN BLOWING YOUR HORN, WILL KEEP ME FROM SLAUGHTERING YOUR TRIBE!
PRRRRAOW!

WHAT DID THAT HORN DO TO SUPERMAN?
HARA CREATED SOME KIND OF ULTRASONIC SOUND.
KLAK KLANK KLIK
IT HURT LIKE HELL.
BUT IT SCARED THE CHEETAH OFF AND IT GOT SUPERMAN STUMBLING. I CAN MIMIC IT--
--AND FOCUS IT ON SUPERMAN UNTIL WE FIGURE OUT WHAT TO DO.
CYBORG STAYS WITH ME. EVERYONE ELSE BRING MINERVA BACK HERE.
THE THREE OF YOU SHOULD--
--HAVE A PLAN. AND I DO.
ON IT.
IF HER TEETH CAN BREAK SUPERMAN'S SKIN, THE CHEETAH'S STRONGER THAN WE THOUGHT.
I'M NOT LEAVING SUPERMAN LIKE THIS. HE CAME HERE TO HELP ME. I HAVE TO HELP HIM.
THE BEST THING TO DO THAT IS TO FIND THE CHEETAH. IF WE'RE GOING TO GET SUPERMAN BACK, WE MIGHT NEED HER.
"AND YOU KNOW THE CHEETAH BETTER THAN ANY OF US, WONDER WOMAN."

<YOUR TRIBE MEMBER CAN'T BE HUMAN. HE'D ALREADY BE DEAD IF HE WAS.>
CAN YOU TRANSLATE, CYBORG?
RUNNING OUR VOICES THROUGH MY SYSTEM NOW. YOU MIGHT HEAR A SMALL ECHO, BUT WE SHOULD BE ABLE TO UNDERSTAND ONE ANOTHER.
HE WAS BITTEN.
HE MUST BE SPECIAL IF HE HAS NOT YET SUCCUMBED TO THE CHEETAH'S ATTACK.
WHAT DID THE CHEETAH DO TO HIM?
FOUND YOU.
BECAUSE I WANTED YOU TO, FLASH.
WE HAVE SEEN THIS BEFORE. SOME VICTIMS HAVE LIVED LONG ENOUGH THAT THEY GO INTO ANAPHYLACTIC SHOCK. THEY UNDERGO A <UNTRANSLATABLE> METAMORPHOSIS.
THEY BECOME ONE WITH THE CHEETAH JUST BEFORE DEATH.
AHHH!
"HOW DO WE *SAVE* HIM?"
"WE MUST ACT QUICKLY."
WE NEED ACCESS TO THE WOUND.

"AND WE NEED TO PRAY TO THE GODS AND GODDESSES OF THESE LANDS THAT HAVE NOT BECOME UNSPOILED AS THE CHEETAH HAS."
SHE TORE MY CALF UP AGAIN. ALMOST CLEAN TO THE BONE.
NNK.
IT'S HEALING, BUT WRONG.
THE BLOOD WILL COUNTERACT THE INFECTION.
STAY HERE AND STAY HIDDEN, BARRY.
NO WAY, DIANA. DOCTORS CAN ADJUST MY LEG LATER. I'M NOT AS FAST, BUT I CAN STILL TANGO WITH THE CHEETAH. WHAT'S THE PLAN?
I DON'T WANT ANYONE ELSE GETTING HURT BECAUSE OF ME.
THE CHEETAH'S CLAWS, NOT YOURS, PRINCESS. SO I REPEAT: WHAT'S THE PLAN?
AQUAMAN WANTS US TO DRAW HER EAST.
"THEN LET'S MOVE."
SUPERMAN IS ONE OF THE MOST IMPORTAN PEOPLE IN THE WORLD.
THIS MAN IS MY FRIEND.
TELL M THIS WIL WORK

THOUGH WE WERE UNABLE TO SAVE MY BROTHER FROM BARBARA MINERVA, WE WILL SAVE HIM.
SHE KILLED YOUR BROTHER?
LAST NIGHT.
"SHE HAS BEEN HUNTING US."
PRRRRAOW!!
I'M GROWING A TASTE FOR YOUR BLOOD, FLASH. JUST AS I HAVE THE SAN TRIBE.
THEY'LL NEVER TAKE THE GODDESS'S POWER FROM ME.
IT'S MINE NOW!
"WHY HAS SHE BEEN HUNTING YOU?"

"BECAUSE WE WANT TO KILL HER."
THE CHEETAH'S DRIVEN YOU MAD BARBARA, BUT YO CAN STILL GET HELP.
YOU CAN STIL GET FRE FROM THI CURSE.
"YOU MISUNDERSTAND WHAT THE CHEETAH IS."

FOR CENTURIES, THE SAN TRIBE HAS HUNTED ALONGSIDE THE CHEETAHS. AND EVERY GENERATION, ONE OF OUR PEOPLE WAS CHOSEN TO BECOME THE HOST OF THE GODDESS OF THE HUNT--THE CHEETAH.
"MY MOTHER WAS THE LAST ONE OF US TO BE SO BLESSED.
"SHE BECAME A GREAT HUNTER FOR MY PEOPLE.
"UNTIL MY MOTHER WAS MURDERED BY A MAN WIELDING THE GODSLAYER--A KNIFE SAID TO HAVE BEEN FORGED BY A BEING SO EVIL, HIS NAME MUST GO UNSPOKEN.
"THROUGHOUT TIME, THE GODSLAYER WAS USED TO KILL MANY OTHER DEITIES--THE LIONESS PAKHET OF EGYPT, THE FRIGID SKADI AND A MYSTERIOUS, ALIEN SUN GOD WHO ANGERED MANY OTHERS.
WHEN I'M THROUGH WITH YOU AND YOUR FRIENDS, I'LL GO AFTER STEVE.
"MY MOTHER DIED TOO... BUT UNLIKE THE OTHER GODS, THE CHEETAH SURVIVED.
"SHE SOMEHOW POSSESSED THE GODSLAYER, CURSING THE HUNTER WHO MURDERED HER.
"THE NEXT BEING THE HUNTER PURSUED WAS YA'WARA--THE CHOSEN JAGUAR GODDESS OF THE AMAZON. BUT YA'WARA BESTED THE HUNTER AND FED HIM TO HER CATS.
"AND FOR A TIME, THE KNIFE WAS LOST.
"UNTIL IT ENDED UP IN BARBARA MINERVA'S HANDS.
THERE IS NOTHING YOU CAN DO HERE, DIANA.
THIS IS MY TERRITORY. WE'RE IN MY ELEMENT.
"AND SHE STOLE THE GODSLAYER."

THEN LET'S GET YOU OUT OF IT.
"AND UNTIL BARBARA MINERVA DIES..."
"...THE CHEETAH IS FOREVER LOST TO US."

"THEY TOLD YOU
MY STORY, DIDN'T
THEY, DIANA?
"THEY TOLD YOU
EVERY LITTLE *DETAIL.*"

SO YOU FINALLY KNOW THE TRUTH.
THE CHEETAH ISN'T THE *BAD ONE.*
*I AM.*
I DON'T BELIEVE THAT, BARBARA.
YES, YOU DO. YOU KNOW I'M AN ANIMAL THAT'S BEEN BAD.
THAT'S WHY YOU PUT ME IN A CAGE.
BUT I LIKE IT HERE.
IT'S WHERE I BELONG WITH THE WORLD THE WAY IT IS.
ONE DAY YOU'LL FEEL DIFFERENTLY.
AND I'LL STILL BE HERE FOR YOU.
FACE THE TRUTH, DIANA!
NOT EVERYONE CAN BE "SAVED"!

NOT EVERYONE WANTS TO BE SAVED...
I'M IN BELLE REVE.
JUST AS YOU REQUESTED.
YES, I CAN WAIT..
JUST TELL ME WHEN BLACK MANTA ARRIVES.
CHEETAH, OUT.

GM7210723
HER NAME IS BARBARA MINERVA NOW, BUT SHE'S GONE BY PRISCILLA RICH, DEBORAH DOMAINE AND SABRINA BALLESTEROS.
EACH ONE OF THESE IDENTITIES IS WANTED FOR MULTIPLE CRIMES, DIANA. FRAUD, THEFT, ASSAULT, EVEN ATTEMPTED MURDER. AND I'D THEORIZE THIS IS ONLY THE TIP OF THE ICEBERG.
SHE KNOWS HOW TO COVER HER TRACKS.
THIS CAN'T BE...
IT IS.
SHE WAS A CRIMINAL LONG BEFORE SHE MET YOU.
THE TRIBE WAS RIGHT, DIANA. THE CHEETAH ISN'T THE ONE WHO CORRUPTED BARBARA MINERVA.
BARBARA IS THE ONE THAT CORRUPTED THE CHEETAH.

MY BEST FRIEND WAS NEVER MY FRIEND AT ALL.
BARBARA WAS RIGHT. I WAS NAIVE. I *STILL* AM.
HOW COULD I HAVE PUT MY TRUST IN SOMEONE LIKE HER? HOW COULD I NOT SEE WHAT SHE REALLY *WAS?*
BECAUSE YOU WERE GIVING PEOPLE THE BENEFIT OF THE DOUBT. YOU WERE LOOKING FOR THE *GOOD* INSTEAD OF THE BAD.
SOMETHING I *ADMIRE* ABOUT YOU.
SOMETHING I TRY TO DO MYSELF.
IF I CAN'T TRUST MY OWN INSTINCTS, I CAN'T TRUST *ANYONE.*
YOU HAVE AN ENTIRE *TEAM* OF PEOPLE YOU CAN TRUST.
YOU CAN TRUST *ME.*
I DON'T KNOW THAT MUCH ABOUT YOU, SUPERMAN.
LET'S CHANGE THAT.

SMALLVILLE DINER
3.99 SPECIAL!!
I DON'T BELIEVE THIS. DO YOU BELIEVE IT?
WELL, OF COURSE I DO!
I CAN'T SEE!
WONDER WOMAN AND SUPERMAN ARE SITTIN' RIGHT THERE! IN OUR DINER!
ASK THEM HOW THEY LIKE MY PANCAKES!
UH, EXCUSE ME, FOLKS. HOW IS EVERYTHING?
IT'S VERY GOOD. THANK YOU.
THANK YOU, MARY.
HOW DID YOU KNOW MY NAME?
HE'S SUPERMAN, MARY! HE KNOWS EVERYONE'S NAME!
I BROUGHT YOU HERE BECAUSE I WANTED YOU TO MEET THE NICE COUPLE THAT RUNS THIS DINER.
AND THE FAMILIES THAT COME HERE.
THIS IS WHY I'M SUPERMAN...

TO PROTECT SMALLVILLE?
TO PROTECT PLACES LIKE THIS.
WHEN WE WERE STOPPING DARKSEID FROM TRANSFORMING THIS WORLD INTO A FIREPIT, OR KEEPING DAVID GRAVES FROM UNLEASHING AN ARMY OF PARASITIC SPIRITS ON THE WORLD, THIS IS THE WORLD I'M FIGHTING FOR.
AND THIS IS WHERE YOU GREW UP?
IT'S WHERE THE ROCKET CARRYING ME FROM KRYPTON LANDED. WHERE THE KENTS FOUND ME. WHERE THEY TAUGHT ME THAT LIFE WAS ABOUT USING YOUR TALENTS TO HELP MAKE THE WORLD A BETTER PLACE.
SOMETHING YOU DECIDED TO DO ON YOUR OWN.
CAN I MEET YOUR PARENTS?
THEY PASSED ON. SOME TIME AGO NOW.
THE FARM'S RUN BY ANOTHER FAMILY WHO LEASES THE FIELDS, BUT I KEPT THE HOUSE I GREW UP IN.
EVERY ONCE IN A WHILE, I NEED TO COME HOME TO REMEMBER.
IT'S BEAUTIFUL, CLARK.

THERE IS LIFE OUTSIDE THE WATCHTOWER. OUTSIDE THE JUSTICE LEAGUE.
AND IT'S A GOOD LIFE, DIANA.
DON'T LET THE EVIL AND CORRUPTION WE BATTLE EVERY DAY MAKE THAT ANY LESS TRUE.
SOMETIMES GOOD IS WHAT IT APPEARS TO BE-- GOOD.
I THOUGHT SO, BUT SOMETIMES THAT FEELS TOO SIMPLE NOW.
SOMETIMES IT'S STILL THAT SIMPLE.
AS SIMPLE AS SMALLVILLE.

END

UNKNOWN SUBJECT
PROBABLE META: BEGIN RECORDING
TARGET DESIGNATE: ANGEL-22
SUBJECT: TREVOR, STEVE

AVAL BASE, CORONADO.
YOU WANT TO DO WHAT?
NAVAL BASE CORONADO
WE WANT TO TAKE HER OFF BASE, INTO THE CITY, SPECIFICALLY...
...DOCTOR MINERVA THINKS IT'LL HELP ACCLIMATE HER TO OUR CULTURE, AND THAT WILL MAKE UNDERSTANDING EACH OTHER EASIER.
MIGHT I REMIND YOU, LIEUTENANT, THAT ACCORDING TO YOUR OWN ANALYSIS, WE'RE LOOKING AT A TERRORIST STRIKE ON AMERICAN SOIL?
I AM AWARE, SIR.
R. MICHAELIS
AND FURTHER, THAT OUR LAST ATTEMPT TO IMPAIR THE SEAR GROUP ENDED WITH THE DEATH OF MISTER TREVOR'S TEAM?
I AM AWARE OF THAT AS WELL, SIR.
IT'S NOT LIKE WE CAN KEEP HER HERE IF SHE WANTS TO LEAVE, MATT.
YOU SAW WHAT SHE DID TO THE BRIG. THAT'S NEW. SHE COULDN'T DO THAT ON THE ISLAND.
ANDY
U.S. NAVY
STEVE--
WHEN SHE TALKS ABOUT THE GREEK GODS VISITING HER, SHE'S TELLING THE TRUTH.
SO NOW YOU BELIEVE IN THE GREEK GODS, TOO?
I KNOW WHAT I'VE SEEN.
CHAELIS
SHE'S HERE WITH US BECAUSE SHE WANTS TO BE, MATT.
SHE'S ON OUR SIDE.
U.S. NAVY
SIX-HOUR LIBERTY, THAT'S IT...

"...BACK ON BASE BY TWENTY-TWO HUNDRED HOURS...."
DARCY
BARBARA ANN! IT IS VERY LOUD!
WHAT'D SHE SAY?
YES, THERE ARE MANY PEOPLE, AND THE STORES--THE SHOPS--USE MUSIC TO ATTRACT ATTENTION.
SHE SAYS IT'S LOUD.
BARBARA ANN, WHY DOES THE AIR TASTE THIS WAY?
WHAT'D SHE SAY?
AH, THAT... THAT'S PROBABLY A MIXTURE OF THE EXHAUST FROM THE CARS AND THE FOOD THAT'S SOLD HERE, THE SUGAR.
SHE'S ASKING ABOUT THE... NEVER MIND.
BARBARA ANN, ARE THERE ALWAYS SO MANY PEOPLE? THERE ARE SO MANY PEOPLE...

YEAR ONE
Part Four
GREG RUCKA Writer
NICOLA SCOTT Artist
ROMULO FAJARDO JR. Colors
JODI WYNNE Letters
SCOTT & FAJARDO JR. Cover
REBECCA TAYLOR Assoc. Editor
MARK DOYLE Editor
WONDER WOMAN Created by WILLIAM MOULTON MARSTON
...MEN AND WOMEN AND, AND... SMALL MEN AND WOMEN, AND THE--THE CHILDREN, AND BABIES...
DO YOU WISH TO LEAVE?
IT CAN BE OVERWHELMING, IT CAN BE TOO MUCH AT ONCE.
NO, NO, IT IS...IT IS GOOD, IT IS...
...WONDERFUL!

WE SHOULD FIND SOMEPLACE TO EAT.
Oh! Oh, CHURROS! WE'VE GOT TO GET HER A CHURRO!
ARE YOU DAFT? THEY'RE PURE SUGAR...
...YOU'LL MAKE THE POOR THING SICK TO HER STOMACH....
AND A MOVIE, WE COULD TAKE HER TO A MOVIE...
...SOMETHING GOOD, IS THERE ANYTHING GOOD PLAYING?
I'M THINKING MEXICAN FOR DINNER...
...DO YOU THINK SHE'D LIKE THAT? OR, WHAT, TOO SPICY?
WE NEED TO FIND A BOOK STORE...
...SOME CHILDREN'S BOOKS TO START WITH...
...BASIC-READER SORTS OF THINGS...
MAYBE WORKING ON SPOKEN COMPRE-HENSION...
...BEFORE WE WORRY ABOUT READING, DOCTOR...
HELLO.

HELLO.
I LIKE YOUR OUTFIT.
I'M REBECCA. THIS IS MY BROTHER, DAVID. HE'S ONLY FIVE.
DIANA.
YOU MAKE FRIENDS EASILY.
THERE ARE NO CHILDREN WHERE I AM FROM.
I WAS THE ONLY ONE.
I'D LIKE TO HEAR MORE ABOUT YOUR HOME.
ARE YOU HUNGRY? WE ARE THINKING ABOUT A MEAL.
DINNER?
DINNER. YES.
PLEASE.
HEY! I UNDERSTOOD THAT!
MISTER TREVOR, WE ALL UNDERSTOOD THAT.

IT'S CALLED A MARGARITA.
MAR-GA-RI-TA.
THESE AREN'T THE BEST YOU'LL FIND, BUT THEY'LL DO FOR AN INTRODUCTION.
YOU THINK GIVING HER ALCOHOL IS A GOOD IDEA?
OPEN
PLEASE WAIT TO BE SEATED
LOOK AT THIS GIRL, STEVEN! YOU THINK SHE'S EVEN GOING TO FEEL ONE MARGARITA?
DIANA? A QUESTION, IF YOU WILL?
THE GODS-- YOUR PATRONS-- YOU SAY THEY GAVE YOU GIFTS. SO YOU COULD HELP. THAT'S WHAT YOU SAID.
DO YOU KNOW WHAT THESE GIFTS ARE?
THEY GAVE OF THEMSELVES TO ME.
AS WE BELIEVE, THE PATRONS GIVE TO US, AND WE GIVE IN RETURN.
WHAT--
WAIT.
BUT WHAT DID THEY GIVE YOU, SPECIFICALLY? ASIDE FROM STRENGTH.
I DON'T KNOW. THEY TOLD ME I WILL LEARN THEM AS I NEED THEM.
SOME GIFTS THEY GIVE ARE CLEAR. OUR HOME. THE LIVES OF MY SISTERS.
OTHERS, THEIR PURPOSE IS TO BE DISCOVERED...

...THIS IS THE GOLDEN PERFECT, GIVEN TO MY PEOPLE BEFORE I WAS BORN.
ITS PURPOSE IS UNKNOWN...
...BUT ITS POWER IS--
--UNMISTAKABLE...
I UNDERSTAND YOU. I UNDERSTAND YOU!
AND I YOU, ETTA CANDY.
TAKE HOLD. BARBARA ANN, TAKE HOLD--
STEVE, GRAB THIS--
YOUR FATHER WAS AN ASS, DOCTOR MINERVA.
YOU HAVE NOTHING TO PROVE TO ANYONE, LIEUTENANT CANDY.

ARGHHHH
KRAK KRAK KRAK KRAK
Oh MY GOD--
GUN! GUN!
ETTA! HOW MANY?
KRAK
KRAK
KRAK
I CAN'T-- ONE, SECOND LEVEL--
--WAIT THERE'S ANOTHER, STAIRS RIGHT--
KRAK KRAK KRAK KRAK KRAK KRAK
--DOCTOR, DIANA, GET DOWN--

KRAKKRAKKRAKKRAKKRAKKRAKKRAKKRAKKRAKKRAKKRAKKRAKKRAKKRAK
--STEVE, WAIT!
GET DOWN, GET--
--DOWN!
KRAK KRAK KRAK
KRAK KRAK
STAY WITH ME, HONEY. STAY WITH ME.
STEVE! STEVE--
--I'VE GOT FIVE, MAYBE MORE! ON EVERY LEVEL!
KRAKKRAK KRAK
NO.

THIS IS NOT A BATTLEFIELD.
PUT THE GUNS AWAY.
HIS WILL SHALL NOT BE DENIED.
I SAID--
--PUT THE GUNS AWAY.
MOMMY!
M--
--OM--

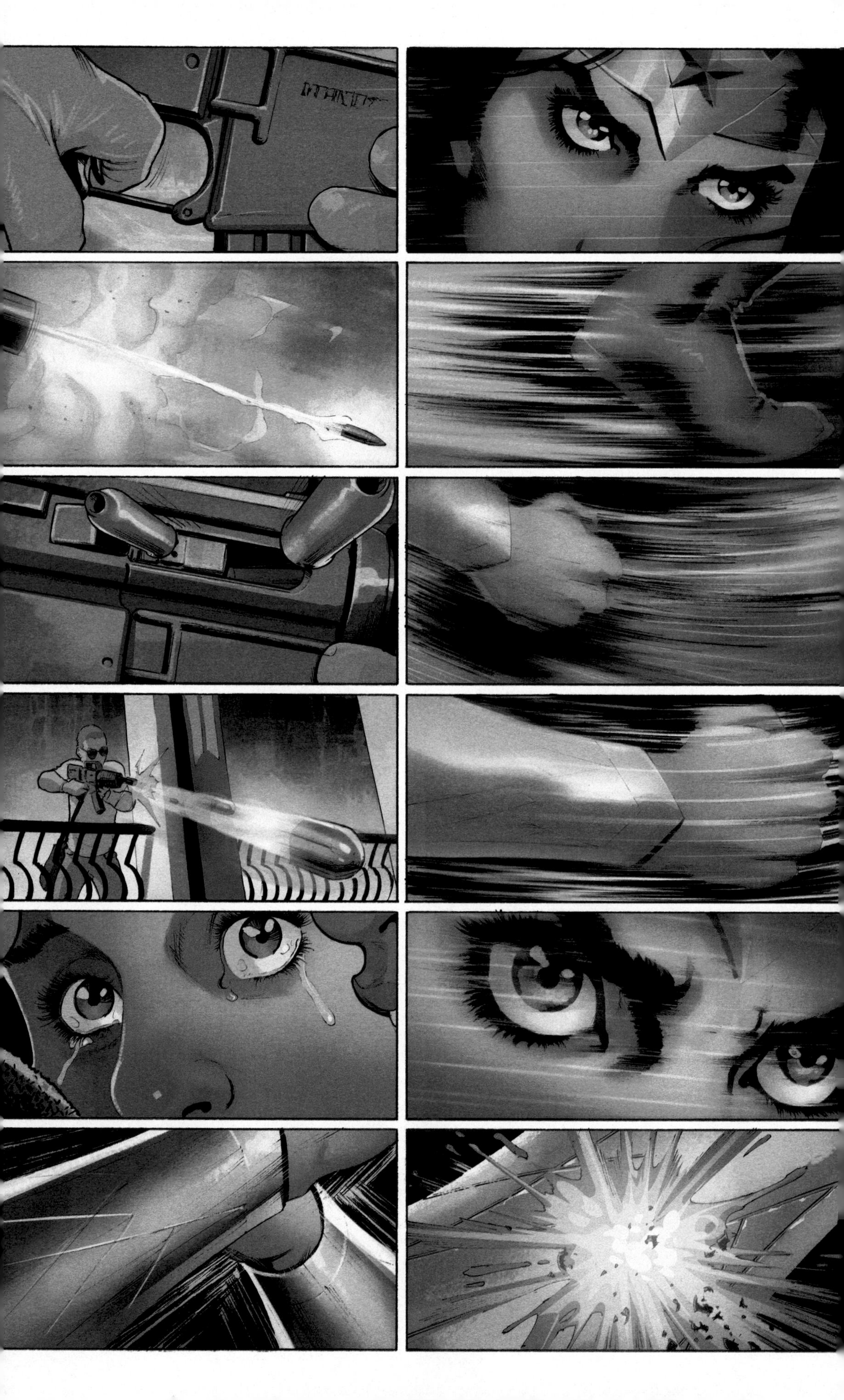

--MMEEEE!!!!
TIME-LA
--MMEEEE!!!!
TIME
00:00:21
--MMEEEE!!!!
TIME-LAPS
PHOTO

--MMEEEE!!!!

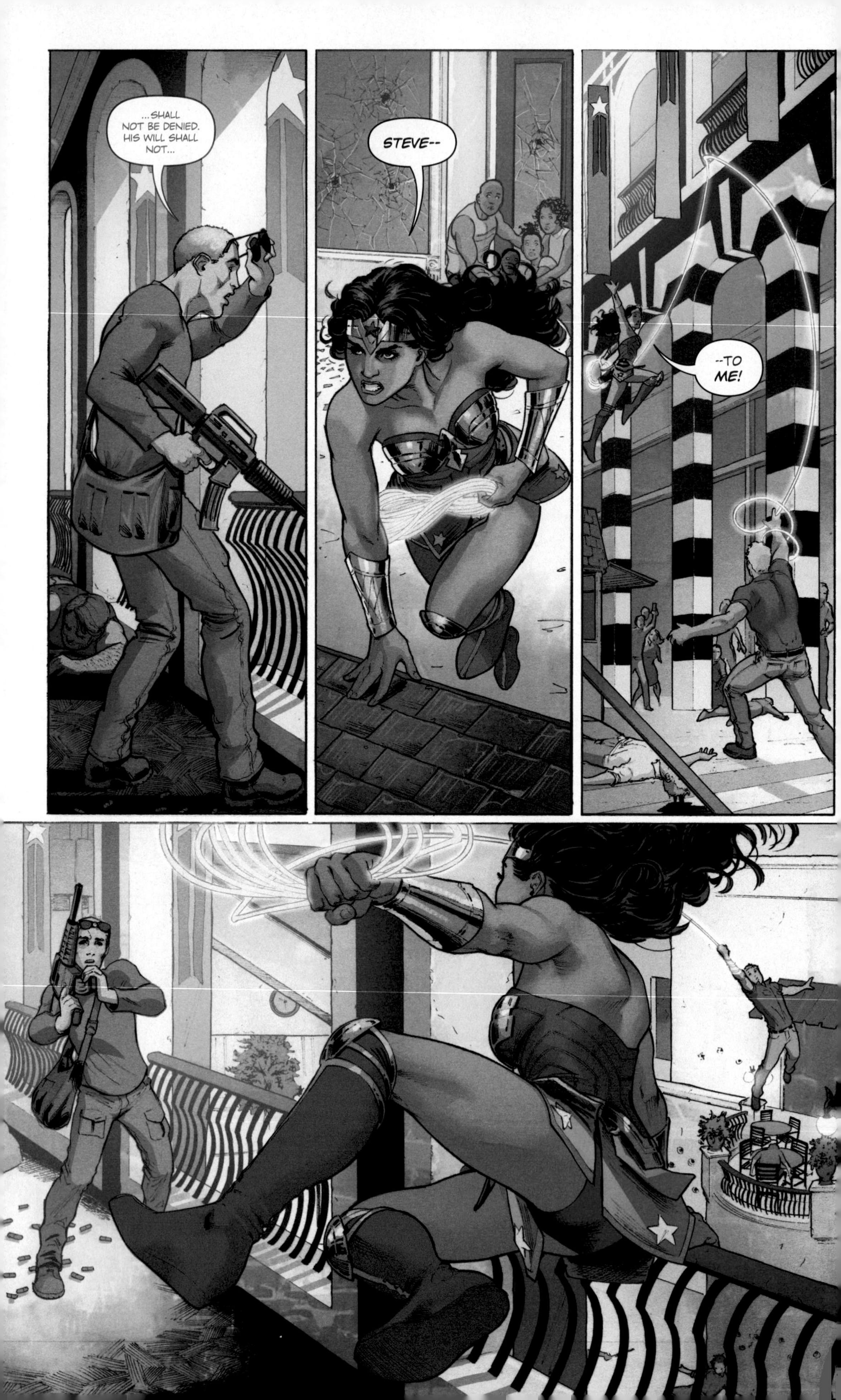
...SHALL NOT BE DENIED. HIS WILL SHALL NOT...
STEVE--
--TO ME!

...DENIED. HIS WILL SHALL NOT BE--
I'M HERE, WE'RE GONNA HELP YOU...
STEVE. ARE MORE?
KRAKKRAKKRAK
ETTA SAID FIVE, SO TWO LEFT!
MIMI'S
WHY DO THEY DO THIS?
WHY DO THEY MAKE THIS A BATTLEFIELD?

THIS IS NOT GOOD!
KRAKKRAKKRAKKRAKKRA
Oh GOD, NO...
...THE GRENADE--
--DON'T LET IT EXPLODE!

KRAKKRAKKRAKKRAKK
ENOUGH.
NO MORE.
--NOT BE DENIED. HIS WILL SHALL NOT BE DENIED--
THE WOMAN! WHERE'D SHE GO, WHERE'D...
...SHE GO...?
MIMI'S
GAB'S

...OVER, IT'S REALLY OVER?
...CAN'T FIND HIM, HE'S NOT ANSWERING HIS PHONE...
...oh MY GOD oh MY GOD...
...SHE IS, DO YOU--
...ANOTHER ONE, THERE'S SO MUCH BLOOD...
LOOK!
LOOK, LOOK AT--
--COUNTED ONE-TEN AND THREADY, BUT I WAS ABLE TO SLOW THE BLEEDING.
NICE, OKAY, WE'LL TAKE IT FROM HERE...
--SEEING THIS, WHO IS SHE--
WE NEED TO FIND STEVE AND DIANA.
NO, WE DON'T.
LOOK UP, LIEUTENANT.
Huh.
DIDN'T KNOW SHE COULD DO THAT.
ETTA, MY DEAR...

...I SUSPECT **SHE** DIDN'T KNOW SHE COULD DO THAT, **EITHER.**
ALL **YOURS,** OFFICERS.
BARBARA ANN, YOU AND ETTA, YOU ARE **UNHARMED?**

WHO ARE YOU?
WHERE DO YOU COME FROM?
WHAT'S YOUR NAME?
ARE YOU ANOTHER ALIEN? WHAT PLANET?
WILL YOU BE MAKING SAN DIEGO YOUR HOME?
HOW TALL ARE YOU?
WHO DOES YOUR HAIR? YOUR CLOTHES?
THERE'S BEEN A TRAGEDY HERE. PERHAPS YOU VULTURES MIGHT WISH TO COVER THAT INSTEAD?
SWAT
LIEUTENANT, MISTER TREVOR, I THINK IT MIGHT BE BEST IF WE GOT OUR FRIEND AWAY FROM HERE...
...THE PRESS HAVE ARRIVED, AND THEY ARE, OF COURSE, FAR MORE INTERESTED IN HER BRA SIZE THAN WHAT'S JUST HAPPENED HERE...
...WHAT?
THE SHOOTERS...
I HAVE SEEN THAT BEFORE....
SO HAVE I.
...IT'S THE SEAR GROUP.
END

NAME'S MASTER CHIEF STEVEN HOWARD TREVOR. FRIENDS CALL ME STEVE.
I'VE BEEN A LOT OF THINGS IN MY LIFE. PAPERBOY. FRAT BOY. SPY. PILOT. MILITARY LIAISON.
CURRENTLY I'M THE HOSTAGE OF "MENINIST" TERRORISTS WHO BROKE INTO A S.T.A.R. LABS BIOTECH FIRM HOPING TO STEAL A CHEMICAL COMPOUND BELIEVED TO MAKE WOMEN SUBSERVIENT.
XY
XY
THROOM
I'M ALSO THE ONLY ONE HERE WHO KNOWS THAT THIS LAB'S MAIN FIELD OF STUDY IS "TRANSPECIES MODIFICATION FOR MILITARY APPLICATION."

I'VE BEEN A LOT OF THINGS. BUT I'M MOST KNOWN FOR BEING *ONE* THING IN PARTICULAR.
I'M THE GUY WHO FOUND *PARADISE*...

...AND BROUGHT A PIECE OF IT BACK.
YOU JUST COULDN'T WAIT FOR ME, STEVE?
WONDER WOMAN?!
HEY, I WAS JUST TRYING TO SAVE THESE DORKS FROM YOU.


WONDER WOMAN'S BOYFRIEND

# STEVE TREVOR IN: THE RIVER OF LOST YEARS

TIM SEELEY writer
CHRISTIAN DUCE artist
ALLEN PASSALAQUA colors
JOSH REED letters
PAUL RENAUD cover
DAVE WIELGOSZ asst. editor
CHRIS CONROY editor
MARK DOYLE group editor
WONDER WOMAN created by WILLIAM MOULTON MARSTON

AND NOW I MUST SAVE THEM FROM AN OUT-OF-CONTROL FROTHING RED PHALLUS.
COULDN'T THINK OF A MORE APPROPRIATE METAPHOR IF I TRIED.
I HOPE THIS DOESN'T INTERRUPT OUR PLANS FOR THIS EVENING.
CHAK
I WAS TO UNDERSTAND THERE WOULD BE DINNER AND WINE FOLLOWED BY FLIRTING, LIGHT TOUCHING, AND SEXUAL TENSION.
SORRY. I'M OVERLY HONEST.

AND WITH MY LASSO OF TRUTH HOLDING YOU TIGHT, SO ARE YOU.
BEEP BEEP
I HATE WOMEN BECAUSE I'M INSECURE AND FULL OF SELF-LOATHING!
OF COURSE YOU ARE.
OH.
STEVE?
I'M SORRY, DIANA. I HAVE TO GO AWAY FOR A FEW DAYS.
CAN YOU TELL ME WHERE?
ONLY IF YOU USE THAT, ANGEL.
GO, STEVE TREVOR.
BUT WHEN YOU COME BACK I WILL EXPECT MY WINE AND TENSION.

CAPPADOCIA REGION, TURKEY.
DIANA KNOWS I HAVE SECRETS. MOMENTS FROM LIVES I LIVED BEFORE WE BECAME AS... CLOSE AS WE ARE NOW.
THAT'S ENOUGH TO BUY SILENCE AS WELL?
YES.
IN ONE OF THOSE LIVES I HEADED A.R.G.U.S.'S* BLACK ROOM FIELD REGIMENT CALLED THE ODDFELLOWS.
* ADVANCED RESEARCH GROUP UNITING SUPER-HUMANS. --CHRIS
THE ODDFELLOWS' FUNCTION WAS TO CLANDESTINELY INVESTIGATE "STRANGE HAPPENINGS" AND DETERMINE IF ANYTHING NEEDED TO BE CAPTURED AND CATALOGED.
OR BLOWN TO HELL.
IT WAS DIFFICULT, DANGEROUS WORK THAT COULD DRIVE A PERSON INSANE.
A.R.G.U.S. FOUND THREE OFF-THE-BOOKS SOLDIERS TO MEET THEM HALFWAY.

ARLIE. EX-BRITISH ARMY
PER. STEADIEST HAND IN
E BUSINESS UNLESS HE'S
AVING A PANIC ATTACK,
HICH IS OFTEN, OR NOT
DRINKING, WHICH ISN'T.
SAMEER. FORMER MOROCCAN INTELLIGENCE. SPEAKS TWENTY-FOUR LANGUAGES AND HE'S A CON MAN IN EVERY SINGLE ONE. HAS A SOFT SIDE, OR HE'S AS GOOD OF AN ACTOR AS HE SAYS HE IS.
"CHIEF." FORMER SHADOW WOLVES SMUGGLER-HUNTER. USED HIS EXPERIENCE TO HELP REFUGEES AND ILLEGAL IMMIGRANTS, BUT WAS EVENTUALLY CAUGHT. JOINED A.R.G.U.S. TO COMMUTE HIS SENTENCE AND TO HAVE AN EXCUSE TO BLOW THINGS UP. AMATEUR JEWELRY DESIGNER.
THEIR STRENGTH WAS THAT THEY WERE MORE DANGEROUS AND WEIRDER THAN THE THINGS WE WERE HUNTING.
HONESTLY, AS THE "GUY NEXT DOOR," I NEVER REALLY FIT IN. BUT THEY WERE MY FRIENDS. AND FOR THEM TO SEND ME THESE COORDINATES WITHOUT EXPLANATION...

...IT MEANS THINGS GOT TOO DANGEROUS AND WEIRD FOR THEM TO HANDLE ALONE.
SUCH A BEAUTIFUL LAND. LITTERED WITH TOWERS THAT LOOK AS IF THEY COULD HAVE BEEN CARVED BY THE DARK ELVES.
NOW IT IS VISITED BY FIERCE WARRIORS WAITING TO DIE BRAVELY IN BATTLE, SO THEY MIGHT BE CHOSEN BY THE VALKYRIE.
IT IS LIKE A FAIRY TALE OF MY YOUTH.
BUT I'M ALL DONE WITH CHILDREN'S STORIES, GIRL. YOU'VE HAD ENOUGH TIME, AND YOUR FRIENDS WON'T LAST MUCH LONGER. TELL ME WHERE IT IS.
OR I WILL MAKE THE VALKYRIE'S CHOICE MUCH EASIER.
FATMA. DON'T TELL SATURNA ANYTHING.

CRIMSON MEN.
FCHOOOOM
AND THEIR LEADER, SATURNA.
A DOOMSDAY MILITIA WHO BELIEVE THE WORLD WILL PERISH UNDER BLOOD RED SKIES.
POK
POK
POK
TOOK YOUR BLOODY TIME, TREVOR!
LIKE A DARK REFLECTION OF A.R.G.U.S., THEY COLLECT THEIR OWN ODDITIES TO PREPARE FOR THE APOCALYPSE.
WHAT, DID SOME SUPERHEROES NEED THEIR UNDERPANTS CHANGED FIRST?
NOBODY MOVE.
PKOW
I'VE GOT THEM, SATURNA--
NO! YOU MIGHT HIT THE GIRL!

THIS CALLS FOR GRACE. AND EXTENDED SUFFERING.
KRAK
WHERE'RE MY SHELLS, CHIEF?!
ALL I CAN FIND IS YER DAFT CRITTER JEWELRY!
DON'T DROP THAT!
WHY'S THAT SO IMPORTANT, THEN?
IT'S A GIFT FOR STEVEN.
WE NEED TO GET FATMA HOME.
WHERE'S THAT?
"FOLLOW THE MOON THE LENGTH OF A SONG TO THE OPEN HAND," SHE SAID.

KRAK
HRNG!
JUST LIKE TREVOR TO GET ALL THE ATTENTION, AY? I'VE GOT THAT BIG BINT.
CHARLIE, YOU'RE SEVERELY WOUNDED, AND YOU HAVEN'T HAD A DRINK IN DAYS.
NO TIME! HEID DOWN, ARSE UP!
DISAPPOINTING. EVEN AFTER ATTAINING RANK YOU ARE STILL JUST A TYPICAL A.R.G.U.S. CUCKOLD. YOU DO NOT EVEN KNOW WHAT YOU FIGHT AGAINST. OR FOR.
GHK!

POK
POK
POK
KRAK
I BLOODY MISSED. AND I'VE ONLY GOT ONE DAMN SHELL LEFT...
NO TIME FOR THAT! SAMEER SAYS THE OLD WOMAN IS FADING FAST! WE NEED TO MOVE!
AS A THANKS, I HAVE MADE YOU THIS, STEVEN.
AH. UH...MUCH APPRECIATED.

WHILE I TRY AND CONTEMPLATE EXACTLY WHAT ANIMAL THIS IS, I COULD SERIOUSLY USE A SIT REP.
WE OWE YOU THAT, IN ADDITION TO OUR LIVES.
FOUR DAYS AGO, WE RECEIVED INTEL ON A CRIMSON SCIENCE DIVISION IN ISTANBUL.
WE TERMINATED THEM, AND THEIR LAB. AND THEN WE FOUND HER.
HER NAME IS FATMA. THREE DAYS AGO SHE APPEARED TO BE SEVEN YEARS OLD.
ALI BABANIN BIR ÇIFTLI I VAR ÇIFTLI INDE HOROZLARI VAR...
...Ü ÜÜRÜ ÜÜ DIYE BA IRIR ÇIFTLI INDE ALI BABANIN...
BY THE FIRST NIGHT AFTER WE RESCUED HER, SHE APPEARED TO BE IN HER LATE SIXTIES. HER SKIN WRINKLED. HER BONES WEAKENED.
SHE SAID THAT ONLY BRINGING HER HOME COULD "STOP THE MANY DAYS FROM FINDING HER."
WE WERE ALMOST THERE WHEN THE BLONDE WOMAN AMBUSHED US.
...ALI BABANIN BIR ÇIFTLI I VAR ÇIFTLI INDE KUZULARI VAR--
SHE STOPPED SINGING.

YES.
THE "OPEN HAND."
AS FATMA LEADS US THROUGH THE WINDING CAVERNS, I GET A SENSE OF DÉJÀ VU.
YEARS AGO, I SURVIVED A PLANE CRASH. I FOUND DIANA AND HER ISLAND OF AMAZONS.
NOW, I'M STUMBLING INTO ANOTHER BEAUTIFUL, SECRET LAND. SECURE. PEACEFUL. HIDDEN FROM THE CORRUPTION OF MAN'S WORLD. NO WANT. NO FEAR.
NO AGING.
SOMEHOW THIS FLYBOY HAS FOUND PARADISE. AGAIN.

FATMA. IÇMELISIN.
IÇMELISIN.
IT'S OKAY. LET THEM TAKE HER.
UH...KIDS KIND OF CREEP ME OUT.
THEY SAY THEY CAN HELP YOU. THEY SAY THEY CAN TREAT YOUR... "OWIES."
FATMA. SHE'S TALKING. WHAT'S SHE SAYING?
SHE SAYS SHE GOT BORED. SHE WANTED TO SEE THE WORLD OUTSIDE THEIR RIVER. SHE SAYS SHE THOUGHT TWO HUNDRED YEARS WAS A LONG TIME FOR ONE PLACE.
"SHE SAYS SHE'S SORRY. THAT SHE MISSED THEM ALL.
"SHE SAYS SHE'S SO HAPPY TO BE HOME AGAIN."
PATHETIC.

YOUR SENTIMENTALITY WILL GET YOU NOWHERE WHEN THE RED SKIES COME.
PUT DOWN THE WEAPONS, PLEASE, OR WE BEGIN SHOOTING.
SURPRISED TO SEE ME, ARE YOU? IS EVEN THE FAMED STEVE TREVOR CAPABLE OF UNDERESTIMATING A WOMAN?
I SUPPOSE YOU COULD BE FORGIVEN FOR NOT KNOWING I AM A MISTRESS OF THE NECROMANTIC ARTS, ABLE TO LIFT MYSELF ON BLACK WINGS AND REANIMATE THE DEAD.
BUT I CAN'T VERY WELL REPOPULATE A MURDERED WORLD WITH WALKING CORPSES, NOW CAN I?
NOW YOU CAN SEE WHY I NEED THIS RIVER AND THESE MAGICAL CHILDREN.
IF YOU WOULD ALL LINE UP NEATLY SO I CAN KILL YOU WITHOUT HITTING ONE OF THE LITTLE THINGS, IT'D BE MUCH APPRECIATED.
YOU'D BE AMAZED AT HOW MANY STREET URCHINS WE HAD TO GO THROUGH TO FIND JUST THE ONE.
Ψάρια βόμβα φωτογραφίστε.

IT TAKES ME A QUARTER OF A SECOND TO REALIZE WHAT SAMEER IS DOING. ANCIENT GREEK. THE ONLY OTHER LANGUAGE THAN ENGLISH THAT I KNOW A FEW WORDS OF, ON ACCOUNT OF DIANA.
HE SAID "FISH BOMB SHOOT."
SOMEHOW...I GET IT.
THAT WAS ALWAYS THE REAL MAGIC OF THE ODDFELLOWS. THE WAY THEY GOT THINGS DONE.
WHETHER IT WAS BY SKILL OR LUCK OR UNCONVENTIONAL THINKING...
...THEY ALWAYS MANAGED TO LINE THINGS UP IN THE END...
PKOW

...EVEN IF IT DIDN'T MAKE SENSE TO ANYONE ELSE HOW THEY GOT THERE.
KA-BOOM
AGHK!
AHHHHH!

PURE DEAD BRILLIANT! I FINALLY FOUND A DRINK THAT WORKS BETTER 'N SCOTCH WHISKEY!
HNG. WELL, NOW AT LEAST I KNOW IT WAS SUPPOSED TO BE A FISH.
IS EVERYTHING YOU'VE EVER GIVEN ME A POTENTIAL BOMB?
OF COURSE. WHY MAKE THINGS THAT DON'T EXPLODE? BORING.
GOOD TO KNOW THAT THE MOOSE STATUE ON MY DESK COULD TAKE OUT THE WHOLE FLOOR.
I THINK IT'S A MOOSE.
SHE WANTS YOU TO DRINK THE WATER AND STAY, CHIEF. TO NEVER AGE WITH THEM.
TELL HER THANK YOU. BUT SHE SHOULD SAVE IT FOR HERSELF AND THE OTHERS.
I'VE LIVED TOO MUCH TO LIVE FOREVER.

WHY CALL ME? WHY NOT A.R.G.U.S.?
I'M JUST ONE GUY.
BECAUSE IF WE TOLD A.R.G.U.S. ABOUT FATMA, ABOUT THIS PLACE, THEY WOULD SEE AN OPPORTUNITY.
SOMETHING TO CATALOG IN THE BLACK ROOM. SOMETHING TO EXPLOIT. TURN INTO A WEAPON.
THEY WOULD RUIN IT. AND IT WOULD BE OUR FAULT.
WE KNEW YOU WOULD UNDERSTAND. WE KNEW YOU WERE ONE OF US.
HE'S RIGHT. I'VE BEEN A LOT OF THINGS IN MY LIFE.
PAPERBOY. FRAT BOY. SPY. PILOT. MILITARY LIAISON.
BUT MAYBE MOST IMPORTANTLY...
I'VE ALWAYS BEEN A LITTLE ODD.

YES. THIS IS WHAT I HAD IN MIND.
I KNOW BETTER THAN TO DISAPPOINT YOU, DIANA.
CARE TO SHARE THE EVENTS THAT DELAYED OUR DINNER?

I--
IT'S NOT THAT I DON'T TRUST HER TO LEARN ABOUT THE EXISTENCE OF THE ODDFELLOWS. OR TELL HER THAT THERE'S A SECRET CITY OF IMMORTAL KIDS SQUATTING BY A STREAM IN TURKEY.

IT'S THAT IF I TELL HER, SHE'LL READ ME. LISTEN TO MY VOICE IN THAT WAY THAT SHE DOES. SHE'LL UNDERSTAND THE PARALLELS.
SHE WON'T EVEN HAVE TO BREAK OUT THAT LASSO TO KNOW THE TRUTH.
THE TRUTH THAT, AS MUCH AS I'M GLAD DIANA IS HERE... AS MUCH AS I'VE BEEN IN LOVE WITH HER SINCE THE MOMENT I SET EYES ON HER...
...I FEEL GUILTY.

GUILTY THAT OF ALL THE PLACES I COULD HAVE CRASHED THAT PLANE, IT HAD TO BE THEMYSCIRA.
GUILTY THAT I STUMBLED INTO AN UNTOUCHED WORLD FREE OF WANT. FEAR. AGING.
GUILTY THAT I BROUGHT THE CORRUPTION OF MAN'S WORLD TO PARADISE.
AND MOST OF ALL, GUILTY...
...THAT I *TOOK* A PIECE OF PARADISE...
...BACK.
END?

OW.
GODWATCH
Epilogue
WONDER WOMAN created by
WILLIAM MOULTON MARSTON
REG RUCKA Writer
ILQUIS EVELY Artist
ROMULO FAJARDO JR. Colors
JODI WYNNE Letters
EVELY & FAJARDO JR. Cover
REBECCA TAYLOR Editor
MARK DOYLE Group Editor
DIANA?
DIANA, IS THAT YOU?
GUESS AGAIN.

DOCTOR CALE.
WAS IT THEMYSCIRA? DID YOU REACH PARADISE ISLAND?
GET OUT OF MY WAY, SIR.
WHERE IS SHE? WHERE'S WONDER WOMAN?
WHERE'S THE GIRL, THE ONE WITH NO FACE?
YOU ARE BLOCKING--
TELL ME!
SORRY. I'M JUST...
...WHAT HAPPENED?
NOTHING GOOD.
DIANA!

I WAS **SO** WORRIED--
I AM FINE, STEVEN.
I'M **SO** GLAD TO SEE YOU, YOU DON'T EVEN **KNOW.**
I WAS **AFRAID** I'D NEVER SEE YOU AGAIN...
...I WAS **AFRAID** I'D **LOST** YOU FOREVER....

YOU'RE NOT GOING TO LOSE ME, STEVEN.
I REALLY LIKE IT WHEN WE DO THAT.
I DO, AS WELL.

WHUPWHUPWHUPWHUP

WOULD'VE BEEN NICE OF HER TO SAY GOOD-BYE.
OR, Y'KNOW, OFFER US A LIFT, AT LEAST.
SHE IS GRIEVING. I CAN UNDERSTAND HER NEED TO BE ALONE FOR A WHILE.

I'M MISSING SOMETHING.
THE YOUNG WOMAN YOU SAW WHO HAD HER FEATURES STOLEN. THAT WAS DOCTOR CALE'S DAUGHTER, ISADORE.
SHE CANNOT. IF SHE LEAVES THEMYSCIRA, SHE WILL BE SPLINTERED AGAIN.
CALE WILL NEVER SEE HER DAUGHTER AGAIN, AS I WILL NEVER SEE MY MOTHER.
BUT I THOUGHT YOU GOT THROUGH, YOU ALL--
SHE IS NOW RESTORED.
BUT SHE DIDN'T COME BACK WITH YOU GUYS.
IT IS AS I TOLD YOU YEARS AGO. THEMYSCIRA IS LOST TO ME.
I CAN NEVER AGAIN GO HOME.
WHERE IS BARBARA ANN?
CHEETAH? NO IDEA, SHE SNUCK OFF AS SOON AS IT TURNED DARK.
SHE CAN TAKE CARE OF HERSELF, DIANA...
...RIGHT NOW IT'S YOU I'M WORRIED ABOUT.
LET'S GET YOU OUT OF HERE.
VERY WELL.
I HOPE SHE WILL BE ALL RIGHT.

LET ME IN.
I HAVE WAITED SO LONG TO MEET YOU...
...PLEASE...
...WILL YOU LET ME IN?

GHHNNN
YOU RRREJECT ME?
SO BE IT.
AMAZON AND GOD ALIKE, YOU WILL KNOW A NEW GOD'S WRRRATH...
...MINE.

HOME OF COMMANDER ETTA CANDY, GEORGETOWN. WASHINGTON, D.C.
...SOMETHING THAT CALE'S COMPANY WAS DEVELOPING FOR THE MILITARY ALMOST A DECADE AGO...
...IT'S ESSENTIALLY A NEURAL-NETWORK-CONTROLLED DRONE THAT COULD BE DISGUISED AS A HUMAN BEING.
COFFEE, BLACK.
THANKS. YEAH, CYBERWALKER. I REMEMBER HEARING ABOUT IT.
THEY WERE KEEPING DIRECTOR BORDEAUX AS THE TEMPLATE ON THE "WALKER," THE DRONE...
...PRESUMABLY USING DOCTOR CYBER AS, WELL, THE "CYBER."
GREEN TEA.
THANK YOU, ETTA.
AND MISS BORDEAUX IS RECOVERING?
SHE WAS SUFFERING FROM DEHYDRATION AND MALNUTRITION. HOSPITAL SAYS SHE'LL BE ALL RIGHT IN A FEW MORE DAYS.
I TALKED TO HER LAST NIGHT, SHE DOESN'T REMEMBER ANYTHING OF THE LAST SIX MONTHS.
AND FERDINAND?
HE LEFT. SAID YOU'D KNOW HOW TO FIND HIM IF YOU NEEDED TO.
YOU SEEM TO BE MISSING YOUR LASSO.
I HAD TO LEAVE IT BEHIND.
THAT'S NOT ALL YOU LEFT BEHIND, THOUGH, IS IT?

YOU SAID YOU'D HELP BARBARA ANN.
WE COULD NOT FIND HER--
HOW HARD DID YOU LOOK?
HEY, TAKE IT EASY, THERE, ETTA--
NO, STEVEN!
BARBARA ANN WAS CURED, SHE WAS BACK, AND THEN CALE MADE HER CHEETAH AGAIN!
AND YOU ABANDONED HER!
MAYBE PUT YOUR FEELINGS FOR HER ASIDE FOR A SECOND, ETTA!
DOCTOR MINERVA MADE A CHOICE, REMEMBER? SHE WENT TO CALE, NOT--
ETTA IS CORRECT.
AND I WILL NOT LET BARBARA ANN DOWN AGAIN.
WHERE CAN I FIND DOCTOR CALE?

--THREE DOZEN FBI WITH SUBPOENAS AND EVERYTHING, VERONICA...
...THEY SEALED OFF THE CYBERWALKER LAB AND SHUT DOWN THE MAINFRAME.
I'M RUNNING PRIMARY PROCESSING OUT OF THE STUTTGART NODE AT THE MOMENT.
WHAT ARE THEY LOOKING FOR?
EVIDENCE. THEY KNOW ABOUT BORDEAUX, WHAT WE DID.
THEY KNOW DOCTOR POISON AND HER TEAM MURDERED CANDY'S PEOPLE AT THE PICKET.
THEY'RE TRYING TO TIE IT ALL BACK TO YOU, VERONICA.
MAKE SURE THE TRANSFERS TO MARU AND TEAM POISON HAVE BEEN SCRUBBED.
THE REST OF IT...LET OUR LAWYERS TAKE CARE OF IT.
I ALREADY WIPED THE MONEY TRAIL, BUT IF THEY FIND ANYTHING, YOU COULD BE LOOKING AT ARREST OR--
I DON'T CARE!

TEN YEARS TRYING TO SAVE MY DAUGHTER, ADRIANNA! TEN YEARS BARGAINING WITH KILLERS AND PETTY GODS! TEN YEARS OF WONDER WOMAN!
AND IT'S ALL FOR NOTHING!
ALL OF IT TO GIVE IZZY TO THE AMAZONS!
ALL FOR NOTHING.
YOU CREATED ME.
I AM NOT NOTHING.
I AM YOUR FRIEND.
YOU'RE NOT ADRIANNA ANDERSON...
YOU'RE AN AI CREATED FROM THE WOMAN WHO WAS MY FRIEND.
...YOU'RE DOCTOR CYBER.
...I SEE.
UNTIL YOU NEED ME AGAIN, THEN, VERONICA...
...I'LL LEAVE YOU TO YOUR MISERIES....

TELL ME...
...DOES IT HURRRT?
ALL YOU'VE DONE, ALL THE LIES AND BETRRRAYALS...
...ALL FORRR YOURRR DAUGHTERRR...
...IS IT KILLING YOU INSIDE, VERRRONICA?

YES.
GOOD.
IF YOU'RE HOPING I'LL REVERSE YOUR TRANSFORMATION, BARBARA ANN, YOU'RE OUT OF LUCK.
THE LAB IS IN LOCKDOWN AND MY OFFICE IS CRAWLING WITH THE FEDS.
SINS CATCHING UP WITH YOU, ARRRE THEY?
IT'S ALL RRRIGHT. THAT'S NOT WHY I'M HERE.
THIS IS WHO I TRRRULY AM, DOCTORRR CALE.
TIME FOR YOU TO ACCEPT WHO YOU ARRRE.
AND WHO AM I?
A VILLAIN.

rrRRA-AAWRRrr
NO--
nNAAHH!!
--RRRRUNNING--
--AWAY!
KSSSH
YOU CAN'T ESCAPE FATE, VERRONICA.
I'VE EMBRRRACED MINE.
TIME TO MEET YOURRRS--
RELEASE HER.

NOW.
MAKE ME, PRRRETTY PRRRINCE--
--HNNUUHH!!
SET ASIDE YOUR ANGER, BARBARA ANN!
THIS WOMAN CAN RESTORE YOU!

HOW DO YOU RRREMAIN SO NAIVE AFTER SO LONG, DIANA?
THAT'S WHY I WANT HERRR DEAD!
AHHHH!!!
NO!

THIS IS NOT YOU, BARBARA ANN!
COME BACK TO US, PLEASE. COME BACK TO ME AND TO STEVE...
...COME BACK TO ETTA.
ETTA...
...SHOULD FORRRGET THE PAST.
WE ARE OUR PASTS, BARBARA ANN.
GIVE ME CALE'S LIFE, AND I WILL GIVE YOU WHAT YOU ASK.
THAT IS NOT AN OPTION.
THEN THIS ENDS ONE WAY, AND SHE WILL BE BUT THE FIRRRST TO DIE BY MY CLAWS!

RRRARRWWL
HUSH, MY FRIEND...
kkHkk khhh
...HUSH...
...AND SLEEP....
hhk hhkk kk

grrRRWWL
HKKK
YOU SAVED MY LIFE.
YES.

WE'RE NEVER GOING TO BE FRIENDS. YOU UNDERSTAND THAT.
I UNDERSTAND WE COULD HAVE BEEN.
I UNDERSTAND THAT YOU SEE WEAKNESS IN THE PLACES WHERE I FIND STRENGTH.
AND I UNDERSTAND SOMETHING MORE.
DO YOU?
THAT YOU WILL ALWAYS BE ALONE, DOCTOR CALE.
END

"Clear storytelling at its best. It's an intriguing concept and easy to grasp."
—**THE NEW YORK TIMES**

"Azzarello is rebuilding the mythology of Wonder Woman."
—**CRAVE ONLINE**

# WONDER WOMAN VOL. 1: BLOOD

BRIAN AZZARELLO with CLIFF CHIANG

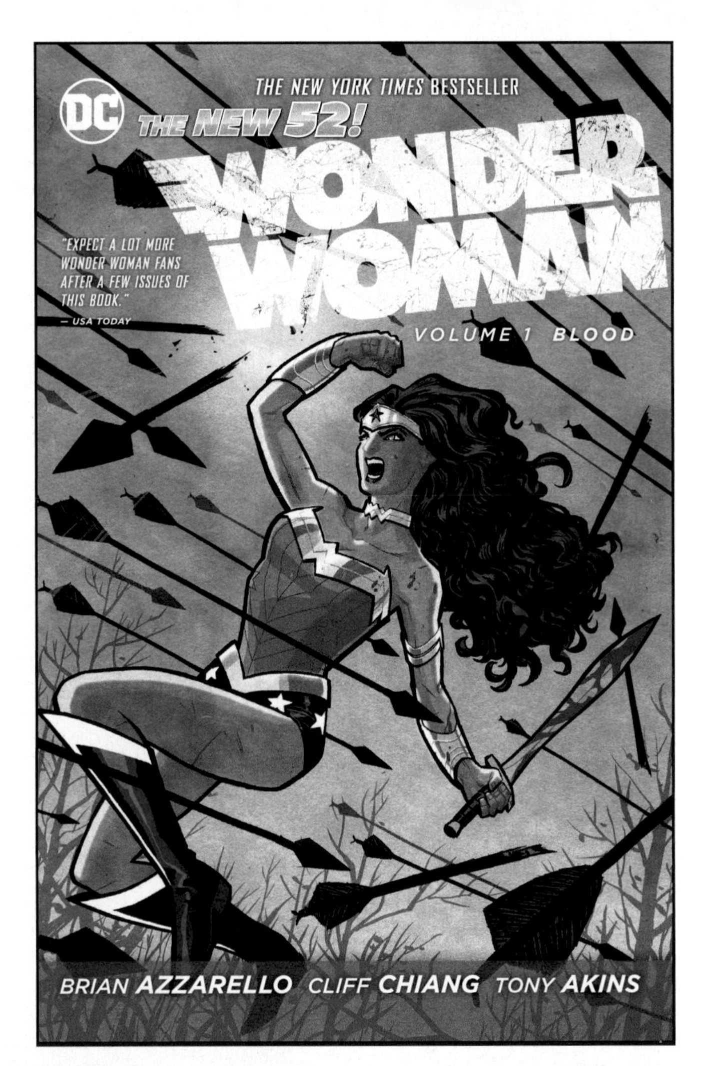

WONDER WOMAN VOL. 2: GUTS

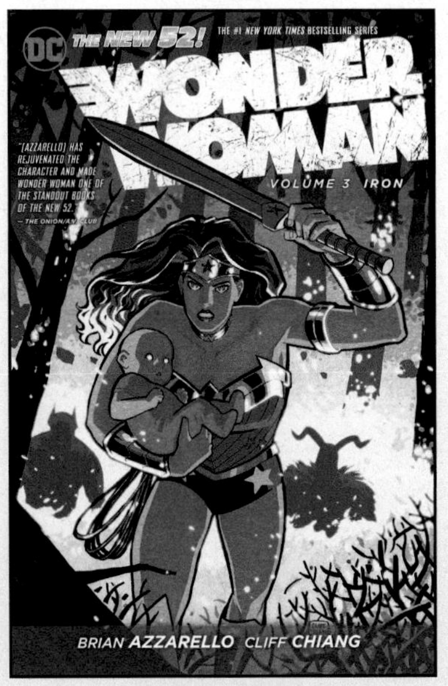


WONDER WOMAN VOL. 3: IRON

## READ THE ENTIRE EPIC!

WONDER WOMAN VOL. 4: WAR

WONDER WOMAN VOL. 5: FLESH

WONDER WOMAN VOL. 6: BONES

WONDER WOMAN VOL. 7: WAR-TORN

WONDER WOMAN VOL. 8: A TWIST OF FATE

WONDER WOMAN VOL. 9: RESURRECTION

Get more DC graphic novels wherever comics and books are sold!

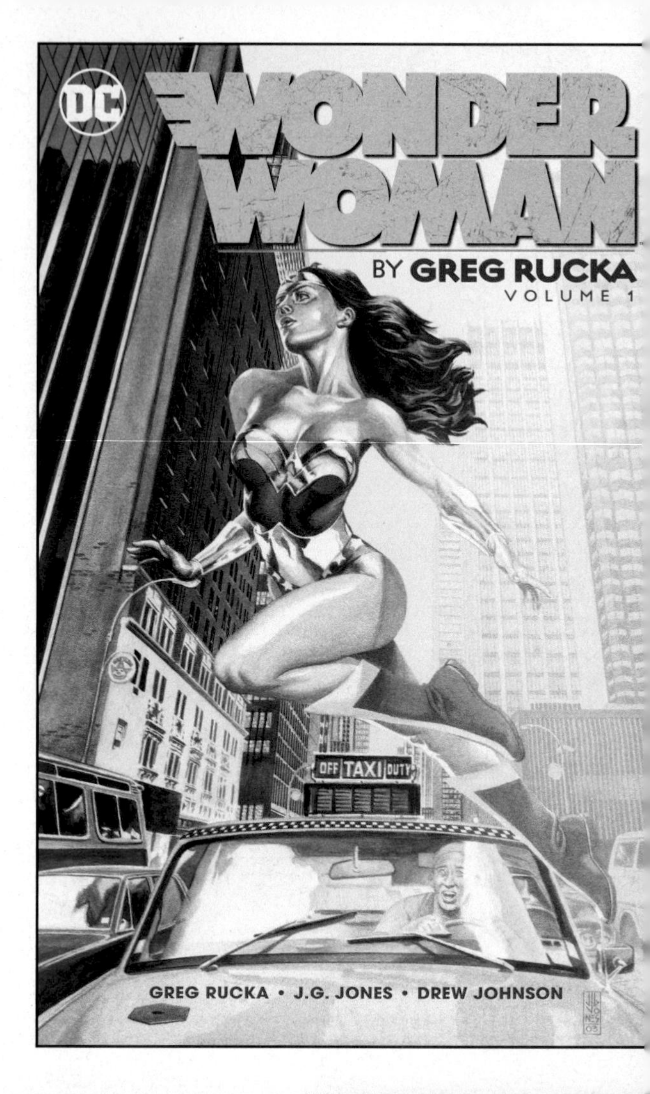


"One of the best writers for Wonder Woman in the modern era."
**– NERDIST**

# WONDER WOMAN BY GREG RUCKA
## with J.G. JONES & DREW JOHNSON

**BATWOMAN: ELEGY**
**with J.H. WILLIAMS III**

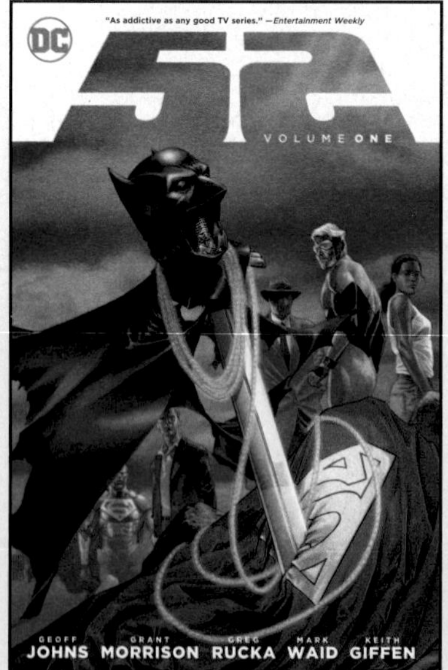


**52 VOL. 1**
**with VARIOUS ARTISTS**

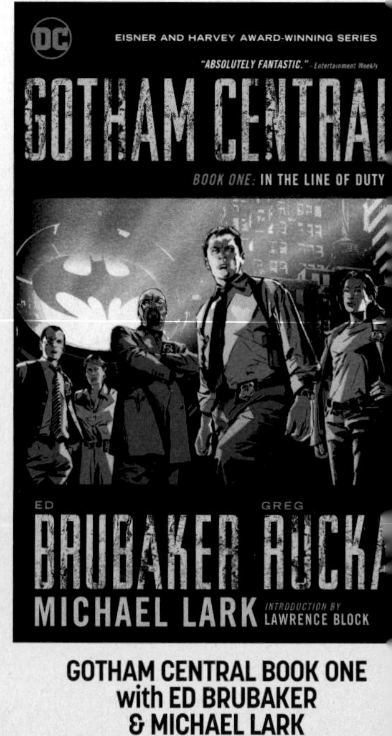


**GOTHAM CENTRAL BOOK ONE**
**with ED BRUBAKER**
**& MICHAEL LARK**

Get more DC graphic novels wherever comics and books are sold!